TN - 65448

DATE DUE

NOV 26 1985			
APR 09 1991			

WITHDRAWN

DEMCO NO. 38-298

149805

Open Education Re-examined

Open Education Re-examined

Editors
Donald A. and Lilian Myers
Oklahoma State University

Lexington Books
D.C. Heath and Company
Lexington, Massachusetts
Toronto   London

Library of Congress Cataloging in Publication Data

Myers, Donald A.
    Open education re-examined.

    Bibliography: p.
    1. Open plan schools—Addresses, essays, lectures. I. Myers, Lilian, joint
author. II. Title.
LB1029.06M93   372.1'3   73-11677
ISBN 0-669-90514-3

Published simultaneously in Canada.

Printed in the United States of America.

International Standard Book Number: 0-669-90514-3

Library of Congress Catalog Card Number: 73-11677

Contents

List of Figures

Foreword

Our educational system, like so many American systems, is under attack. Schools are being challenged from all sides—students, parents, teachers, administrators, and school committees. In this turbulent climate everyone is searching frantically for new and better forms of education. This quest is especially difficult because there are almost as many conceptions of quality education as there are persons in education.

Unfortunately, in the heat of vehement and sometimes violent opposition to public schools, critics seem to be more clear about what they don't like than what they do. Alternatives are frequently accepted enthusiastically and uncritically simply because they promise something other than the status quo. How new plans differ and what will be their effect upon children's cognitive and personal development are questions seldom asked, let alone answered. New is simply accepted as better than old.

Many of the new reforms prescribed for the public schools are spawned by writers, scholars, critics, and professors far removed from students and schools. This is both good and bad. It is good because it permits and encourages fresh, independent, and creative solutions to old problems. It is bad because the further one is from the classroom the more simple his solutions to classroom problems tend to become. (While the closer one is to children in a learning context, the more complex, muddled, and inscrutable both problems and solutions become.)

Most critics outside the schools compare the *best* of what they like with the worst of what they oppose—ripe apples with rotten oranges. Using this approach, open education is better than traditional education or, for that matter, any other form of education. While dramatic and appealing, this posture can be dishonest, simplistic, irresponsible, and, worst of all, destructive. It encourages condemnation of our schools which obstructs and limits what they can accomplish. Furthermore, educational prophets who promise the moon have usually delivered but a piece of cheese. Parents and teachers led to expect unrealistic and unattainable solutions to their problems become only more disappointed, disillusioned, and bitter. In the final analysis, neither heated opposition nor repeated disappointment serve the best interests of children.

Open Education Re-examined is a thoughtful, comprehensive treatment by six educators who are not caught up in uncritical condemnation of our educational system or in uncritical advocacy of open education. They examine open education through lenses well grounded in diverse backgrounds and disciplines. The lenses project a sharp and seldom distorted image. They have no ax to grind, but they do subject open education to an objective, dispassionate, searching (and sometimes painful) appraisal. This kind of sober, intelligent analysis is badly needed at this time. We need to be reminded—as this book does—that being critical is not necessarily being negative; being objective need not mean lacking values; being scholarly does not mean being remote and irrelevant; and being rigorous is not being old fashioned. Unfortunately, too few of the starry-eyed proponents of open education have open minds. They are idealists and evangelists who do not like their causes scrutinized. Most who need to read this book probably will not; those who will read it probably need it less.

Open education is shrouded in vagueness. Neither proponents nor opponents seem able to get a clear handle on it. The question of definition, "what is open education?", is forthrightly addressed here. Clarification is no mere academic exercise because loosely defined concepts and ideologies attract people who "do their own thing," which often distorts if not destroys the original conception. This is a problem of *lack* of definition.

The problem of definition is equally great. As the authors point out, change in American education has usually followed a formula: define in detail what it is you wish to accomplish—the way things *should* be—then set out to make classrooms, children, teachers, and schools be that way. Open education, like its many predecessors, is following this apparently logical pattern.

Unfortunately, trying to achieve a one to one correspondence between any particular classroom and an official "open classroom" creates two fundamental problems: you have to define what an open classroom is, what it contains, what the teacher and children do there; secondly, the more successful you are at definition and description the more likely you will impose these ideas and practices upon children and adults.

Since much of open education seems to be intuitive, personal, idiosyncratic, almost existential in nature, it tends to defy definition. To the extent open education can be identified, attempts to impose it upon children and teachers are seldom pleasant or possible. This is the dilemma of open education and of open educators upon which much light is shed in the following pages. What many seek in open education is a replication of the good things undeniably happening in British primary schools. Yet definition and imposition are antithetical to the British experience. On the contrary, the characteristic most central to the success of good British schools is that the teacher's role and classroom evolve from within, as a function of his observations of children's behavior and of his personal educational beliefs and values. Neither the classroom nor the teacher's behavior are a response to an orthodoxy, to the prods of educational critics, or to the fashionable rhetoric of the day. Our attempts to emulate British classrooms by adhering to the traditional formula for educational change suggest that Americans are neither capable of observing and deriving much meaning from children's behavior, nor are we very certain of what we believe about children and the process whereby they learn. This is a disturbing self-indictment.

There will always be a lack of agreement about what open education is. Attempts to more carefully refine and define its essence—unlike attempts to clarify the nature of the molecule or the solar system—will not result in a clearer and richer concept, for the simple reason that open education does not exist. It does not lie there awaiting our discovery. To the contrary, those who are most carefully defining and describing open education are, by so doing, creating it. One of the virtues of this book is that it asks of us, as it asks of itself, "what is open education?", "what is the difference between open education and good education?", "how is it that many teachers who would not call themselves "open" are outstanding practitioners?", and "how is it that every school system has teachers of open classrooms who are dreadful?" These are not merely questions of semantics and definition. They are questions which get to the root of the educational process itself, of what we are doing, why we are doing it, and of the consequences of what we do. Raising and grappling with questions such as these is long overdue. This may well be the lasting contribution of open education and of this book.

Roland S. Barth

Introduction

I'm growing wary of slogans like open education. So is Barth. I think they may do more harm than good. Currently I'm seeking to enlist everybody in favor of open, informal schooling into a movement whose one slogan will be a demand for decent schools.

> Joseph Featherstone, "Foreword," in Roland S. Barth's *Open Education and the American School* (New York: Agathon Press, Inc., 1972), © by Roland S. Barth, p. x.

On August 19, 1967, an article entitled "Schools for Children: What's Happening in British Classrooms,"[1] by Joseph Featherstone, appeared in a magazine with a circulation of 120,000. This article produced only mild ripples among the readers, since it appeared in the middle of August when vacations were in full swing and magazine reading was at a minimum.

On September 2, 1967, another article "How Children Learn"[2] appeared on the same subject by the same author. This second installment went unheralded, as readers found themselves caught up in end-of-summer activities and the preparation of children for school.

The day after Labor Day, more than 43 million children and 2 million teachers returned to their classrooms. Colleges and universities soon opened for the autumn term. The stage was set for a third article which appeared on September 9, 1967, "Teaching Children to Think."[3]

With the commencement of school and the reemergence of education as a central concern, these three articles soon became the focus of discussion for thousands of persons interested in improving elementary education in the United States. The articles were in such demand that *The New Republic* quickly packaged them together at a price of fifty cents. The response was overwhelming.

Dr. G.W. Bassett, dean, Department of Education, University of Queensland, Australia, was making one of his frequent visits to America to study schools and was astonished at how news of the articles swept the education community from coast-to-coast. He noted that in England (where he had recently spent several months visiting schools), innovations of such magnitude evolved gradually and were often supported by official government reports.[4] Could an innovation be started with a series of three articles, the author of which was virtually unknown to educators?[5]

Six years have elapsed since the publication of these articles. During this time, innumerable articles and dozens of books have been written on the subject of open education. Prestigious "think tanks" like the Educational Development Center, Educational Testing Service, and Stanford Research Center have research projects in this area. Many prominent educators have felt obliged (even compelled) to make a pilgrimage to Oxfordshire, Bristol, and Leicestershire.[6] In addition, many schools of education have offered conferences and workshops in open education, often including visits to England.

One indication of the popularity of open education can be found in the attendance figures of a one-day conference on open education sponsored by the Bureau of Elementary Curriculum Development, New York State Department of Education on December 7, 1970. By count, 2,117 teachers attended this conference sitting with their coats on in an auditorium that was very poorly heated. The temperature outside ranged from a low of six to a high of twenty-five.

The research community was not far behind. By 1973, fifteen persons delivered papers on some aspect of open education at the Annual American Educational Research Association Conference in New Orleans. Inevitably, courses entitled "Open Education" have found their way into the bulging catalogs of colleges and universities. Some virtually unknown schools of education, such as the University of North Dakota, have become overnight successes with the ability to draw talented teachers and graduate students from throughout the nation.

This frantic popularity has been generated by a phenomenon that has yet to be defined as a distinct concept. Indeed, it may never be a concept but remain a set of best existing practices imbued with the aura of an ideology.

In writing this book, we were guided by the timely advice of Mauritz Johnson. In Chapter 1, he states that "criticism too often connotes rejection rather than the exercise of careful judgment," and that even the most evangelistic proponent would not advocate uncritical acceptance of his proposal. This book, then, is an effort to critically examine various aspects of open education.

The authors are diverse in terms of academic affiliation and specialization, political philosophy, and individual temperament. One is a hard-nosed curriculum specialist with a background in mathematics and logic. Another sat in the classes of William Heard Kilpatrick at Teachers College and heard progressive education espoused by overzealous graduate students who later presided over its demise. One is a brilliant young man who emphasizes neither the past nor the present, but a future in which parent-controlled alternative schools will flourish in a more egalitarian society. Another is a practitioner in the best sense of the word—a person who works directly with children, teachers, and administrators—and has a firm grasp of the theory that underlies her actions. One has a varied research background that brings to his analysis a strong foundation in administration, curriculum, and sociology. Finally, one author has spent much of her time observing a faculty grapple with the many problems of opening a school. Suspicious of many things educational, she brings a critical analysis that is too often lacking by those who investigate open education.

The authors have one thing in common. They have been actively involved in classrooms gathering empirical data upon which to base their judgments. Jenny Andreae was born in Great Britain and has taught in elementary schools there and in America. She is a teacher-trainer consultant on open education and is presently Director of Advisory Service, the Teachers Center at Greenwich, Connecticut. She has worked closely with the Educational Testing Service Research Department and with Lillian Weber. Joseph Leese has traveled extensively in Great Britain and visited classrooms there long before they were dubbed "open" by Americans. He has just returned from a four-month visit participating in a joint program of teacher education in open education between Manchester University and the State University of New York at Albany. Daniel Duke and Donald Myers spent much of the 1971-72 school year visiting open education classrooms throughout New York State. In the past school year, Daniel Duke has visited over 50 alternative schools east of the Mississippi, focusing his attention on the sociological factors that explain the current dissatisfaction with conventional public education. Lilian Myers has observed open education classrooms in New York State and specifically one faculty as it attempted to begin an open school. She was also instrumental in coordinating an open education conference in Albany in 1972. While Mauritz Johnson has also visited classrooms, his strength lies in working with many doctoral students who conduct studies concerning educational practices in schools.

Chapter 1, by Mauritz Johnson, offers what amounts to a skeptic's classical and scholarly view of open education. Johnson readily admits to a general ignorance of everything educational, especially open education, but this "ignorance" serves to support his objectivity and reinforce his analysis.

Chapter 2, by Joseph Leese, is a straightforward rebuke to those who refuse to examine the historical antecedents of an educational innovation. He recapitulates the mistakes made in the past as a warning to open education enthusiasts, so that they might avoid embarrassment by making statements identical to those made more than a half century ago.

Chapter 3, by Jenny Andreae, draws from years of experience working with hundreds of teachers and students. Like most British teachers who support Piaget because he provides research to support what they already believe, Andreae does what seems intuitively right drawing from the work of researchers. Her analysis deals primarily with stages in implementing open education, suggesting that there are two major patterns involved.

Chapter 4, by Lilian Myers, presents a balance to the Myers and Duke study in Chapter 5. While they surveyed over a hundred classrooms throughout the state, she observed one elementary school and recorded the difficulties of opening a school. Her report would qualify for the *Journal of Educational*

Autopsy, so often advocated by the late Ole Sand. She concludes with thirteen generalizations which constitute valuable guidelines for those who propose to begin an open school.

Chapter 5, by Donald Myers and Daniel Duke, focuses upon open education at the state level. They report on the status of open education in the State of New York—a state that has an education commissioner who enthusiastically supports open education and is the home of Lillian Weber's experimental open corridor schools in New York City. In all, they visited 122 elementary school classrooms, assessing their degree of openness by using the thirteen criteria of open education derived from authorities in the field.

Chapter 6, by Daniel Duke, is an attempt to understand the societal forces that have encouraged recent educational change. While his analysis is concerned with the broad issue of alternative schools, there is reason to believe that much of it could apply to open education as well. His analysis draws heavily upon sociological ideas, but is reinforced with empirical data gathered from visits to numerous public and nonpublic alternative schools.

Chapter 7, by Donald Myers, identifies and analyzes major problems that are likely to confront open education in the immediate future—definition, adoption, curriculum, teachers, parents, and students. His conclusions are drawn from related research and from his own research and experience.

In critically examining open education, we will no doubt be accused by some persons of trying to be the first to get atop the counterbandwagon of open education, although the literature is already sprinkled heavily with many articles of caution. We will also doubtless be accused of being mere critics who lack the imagination and courage to advocate anything. Such accusations, however, would be false. In general, we support innovations such as open education, nongrading, team teaching, and process learning. But we recoil at the sight of enthusiastic and dedicated teachers embarking on yet another mission that will sap their energy and tarnish their hopes, as it becomes gradually apparent that the concept they seek to establish is defined so poorly and advocated so uncritically, that success will escape all but those extremely talented teachers who succeed in spite of any educational innovation.

This book is dedicated to those who welcome constructive criticism from sympathetic spokesmen of open education.

Donald Myers
Lilian Myers

A Skeptic's View

Mauritz Johnson

The best advice for anyone who is alarmed about a growing movement in education is to ignore it, like a misbehaving child, and it will soon subside and pass into oblivion. Chances are that it will be no more effective than previous endeavors and hence unlikely to do very grave harm (nor any great good, either). To exercise such restraint and patience is difficult, however, because there is always the danger that the zealots who are caught up in the new wave just might convert vast numbers of adherents if no one speaks up to denounce them. Guardians of orthodoxy cannot rest when heresy is afoot. Who can stand idly by when traditional values are threatened and proven ways are discarded?

The Importance of Skepticism

In this dilemma, in which conflict seems inevitable, there is another maxim which can readily be invoked: No program is as good as its proponents hope it is, nor as bad as its opponents fear it is. This applies to both the conventional program and its innovative rival.

Yet no matter how good a program is, it can presumably always be improved, and no improvement can come about without change of some sort. Inertia favors the status quo as most people require persuasion to change. In other words, any reason for inaction is good enough. It is for this reason that one hesitates to raise objections to any new educational proposals. Each argument advanced becomes someone's reason for inaction, or as Duke suggests, "a self-fulfilling prophecy."[1]

On the other hand, it should be possible to assume that no one, even the most evangelistic proponent, advocates *uncritical* acceptance of his proposals. Criticism too often connotes rejection rather than the exercise of careful judgment. The original meaning of "skepticism" is thoughtfulness, not incredulity or doubt.

If the position adopted by the critic or skeptic turns out to be negative with respect to some advocated innovation, it does not necessarily represent either an endorsement of the status quo or a resistance to change. An opponent of a particular innovation must not be assumed to be against change; he may be an enthusiastic proponent of another kind of innovation. Moreover, those critics of current conditions who go beyond mere polemics to put their proposed alternatives into actual practice, must expect those alternatives themselves to become targets for criticism and then they, too, must judge which criticisms are informed and responsible and, hence, useful.

The Elusive Target

Consider how a skeptic might view the phenomenon known as "open education." His first reaction is to the term itself. Most of us are quite sensitive about educational slogans, and are particularly suspicious of any adjective in front of the word "education." In the course of a single career some of us have lived through "progressive education," "life adjustment education," "space-age education," "process education," and "humanistic education" as well as education *for* living, *for* democracy, *for* excellence, *for* a changing world, and so forth.

It is particularly difficult to identify the referent for open education, to know whether a given manifestation is or is not an instance of open education, and in fact to distinguish "open" education from "informal" education (the term Silberman[2] uses) and from "humanistic education," another expression currently in vogue. In the New York State Education Department's Title I Handbook, open education is described (1) in terms of human relations, in which it means mutual trust; (2) in architectural terms, in which it means no partitions; (3) in temporal terms, in which it means a flexible schedule; (4) in terms of teacher personality, in which it means sensitivity and supportiveness; (5) in curricular terms, in which it means something like contingent choice; and (6) in terms of educational goals, in which it implies the cultivation on the part of children of optimistic perceptions of themselves, other people, and material aspects of their environments.[3] Furthermore, in a carefully conducted study, Walberg and Thomas found that open education classes differ from traditional classes in the great diversity of manipulative materials, student self-discipline and student-made materials, student-corrected work, individualized instruction, and criterion referenced evaluation.[4]

On the one hand, if all of these interpretations are correct and all of these features (and more) are *essential* to open education, then we have an enormously complex concept to assess. And objection to any one feature or interpretation results in the rejection of the whole idea. On the other hand, if the various interpretations are alternatives, and if the features are not all "essential" but rather typical or desirable, then we have no coherent concept to deal with at all.

A Slogan for All Seasons

As a slogan, the term open education has much to recommend it. "Open" is no esoteric, exotic, or contrived word. It is a good, common, four-letter Anglo-

Saxon one. Moreover, it has many good connotations: we like an open society, not a closed one; we like open minds, not closed ones; we like people to be open-handed in preference to either tight-fisted or closed-fisted; open-heartedness is preferred over cold-heartedness; we favor open-door policies over restrictive ones, and open-end agreements and open-end test questions because they permit broad interpretations. "Open" goes with "free," and freedom is a good thing. We now think that even universities should have open admission policies. In England, the external degree program is called the open university. So the term is familiar, and it is good. Above all, it is vague and, hence, it is an ideal slogan.

As general advice to administrators, teachers, and students, the admonition to "open things up" is probably as sound as any for dealing with situations in which people are "uptight" where the atmosphere is characterized by pettiness and restrictiveness. Whenever we act as if there is only one way to do anything in schools and as if we have any final answers, we need to be reminded that most, if not all, of our procedures are still open to questions begging for creative invention and careful experimentation. There is nothing dangerous about advocating open education. But saying this may also be suggesting that the idea is innocuous and that little good will come of it. Still, while this particular idea may be fraught with little danger, "a too hasty acceptance of idealistic slogans as a substitute for proven basic educational concepts can lead to educational chaos."[5]

Protect Us from Our Friends

Any idea that is powerful and has potential effectiveness must be coupled with certain cautions to be observed while applying it. One caution concerns the avoidance of extremes. When an idea is carried too far, it often becomes ridiculous and people turn against it. Excesses are most likely to occur when practitioners do not fully understand the idea they are implementing. If some of the features associated with open education were carried to excess, the result would be chaos. With a concept having such a multiplicity of features, there is the related danger that schools will claim to have open education if one or two of its features are present. Nothing dissipates a new proposal faster than having everyone claim, "We're doing that already." Taken together, the overzealous application and the tokenistic appropriation of an idea, on the part of its alleged supporters, are perhaps more inimical to it than anything its critics can come up with.

It cannot be assumed, however, that whenever an idea goes awry in practice, the fault lies in the indiscretion or insincerity of its practitioners. The idea itself may have serious shortcomings. "An inadequate theory of what you are doing is bound to let you down even though your practice may in some measure remedy the defects in your theory."[6]

If some theories are plagued by foolishness in their application, others are rescued by common sense. Internal contradictions within theories are troublesome enough, but they can be minimized, if not resolved, by judicious practice. Educational theories couched in vague phrases not clearly identifying educational aims are virtually impossible to implement. As one British writer put it, "refusal to reflect upon aims does not allow one to escape from actually having them."[7] Finally, no amount of common sense can salvage theories grounded in dubious premises, such as nostalgic views of childhood or romantic notions about the natural state of man.

There are some aspects of open education that critics are unlikely to attack. They are not likely to object to greater trust and mutual respect in relations between teachers and students. They are not likely to object to attractive, inviting room arrangements, or the practice of having a variety of stimulating materials available to children instead of locked away in closets. They will not care whether full partitions or lower room dividers are used, though some may be concerned if children are denied any opportunity for privacy and quiet contemplation. No one will oppose efforts to promote creativity, to enhance self-awareness, to cultivate sensitivity to others, or to foster a sense of community. They might, however raise questions about the following aspects of open education: (1) the educational level at which it is being most vigorously promoted, (2) the concept of childhood that underlies it, (3) the role advanced for the teacher, (4) the implicit reverence for informality, and (5) the treatment of activities as ends.

Misplaced Emphasis

Because of American captivation with developments in the British infant school, open education seems to be identified most closely with the primary grades. Yet it is in primary classrooms that the greatest number of open education features are already found in many American schools—attractive displays, interest centers, intraclass grouping, varied activities, readiness experiences, projects, and multiadult contacts through specialist teachers. This is not to say that these features are found as extensively as they might be and probably should be. As the studies cited by Myers and Duke show, they are all too often lacking, even at the primary level. Nevertheless, they do exist where open education does not, and they are more common in primary classrooms than at higher levels. It is not in these early grades where one finds the largest numbers of bored, alienated children. At this level, interests have not yet become sharply differentiated, and most activities a teacher suggests are likely to be accepted with enthusiasm. By the same token, children at this level are probably least well qualified to make intelligent decisions about what is important for them to learn. British infant schools may be just now arriving where American schools were thirty years ago, and open education advocates may be barking up the wrong tree by emphasizing that level.

Even British observers ask, however, "But how many primary schools have, in recent years, been conducted in a rigid, repressive way?"[8] Skeptics with any sense of educational history cannot accept the assumption of so many would-be reformers that things could not be worse. Things clearly have been worse, and they could be worse yet if the wrong changes are made. Even a veteran critic of American education rejects the premise that American schools are "grim, joyless places."[9] Far from being obsessed with "the cognitive at the expense of the affective," notes Koerner, the schools "are regarded by many people, especially parents, as entirely too permissive and undirected."[10]

If the existence of rules, requirements, standards, order, schedules, routines, and criticism makes the school a repressive institution for the hypothetical child existing free in a state of nature, then the absence or neglect of these features makes the school a fantasyland in the context of the world in which the real child must soon be prepared to live as an adult. It might be well, indeed, if the secondary schools, in which increasing numbers of students appear to chafe at being treated too much like children, could allow greater latitude for individual choice and independent action. But prerequisite to such freedom is a command of skills and an inner discipline. The skeptic wonders whether the adoption of open education in the elementary schools will make more or less likely the development of intellect and character which is essential for greater openness at the secondary level. The notion that permissiveness prepares one to escape or resist repressiveness lacks convincing support.

The Reality of Childhood

The romantic Rousseauian notion of following nature as revealed by the child has been amply and capably criticized, but it has great sentimental appeal and keeps reappearing. One might conclude then that the notion must have some merit and, of course, it does. Skillful teachers observe children carefully and get many cues from their reactions as to the most appropriate approach to follow. But while these road signs help point the way, they should not determine the destination. Children do not, of course, grow up in nature, but in a culture and into adult status in a society. If the hard-won, valuable aspects of that culture are not to be lost, their transmission must be carefully planned and skillfully carried out.

In this undertaking, teachers bear a responsibility to society that should not be shifted to children and their natural inclinations. Indeed, a major aspect of the educative process involves the suppression of natural tendencies in the course of becoming human. Even if one could depend upon every child's eventually developing an interest in acquiring the most essential human capabilities, the brief time available does not permit the luxury of waiting for the interest to manifest itself. And, ironically, the choices which a child might appear to make autonomously must be based on values derived from the culture.

Proponents of open education must recognize that whatever learning environment they may advocate, it too is a cultural creation reflecting one set of culturally derived values. The learning environment may cater to different inclinations on the part of a child, but these inclinations are no more (or less) natural than those encouraged in another setting. In a society in which individual autonomy, choice, independence, creativeness, and originality were not valued, the schools could not promote these values. Moreover, as Peters has pointed out, citing Whitehead's dictum that "autonomy follows precision," in order for children to decide what sort of selves they want to be and know what options are open to them, they must be equipped with literature, history, and other knowledge which only the culture can provide.[11] "Young children cannot be regarded as fully fledged autonomous agents," argues another British skeptic. He continues with the observation that while it is obvious that autonomy develops progressively, it is by no means clear that abundant free choice promotes its development better than direction.[12]

Perhaps these comments misrepresent the view of childhood on which open education rests. But skeptics detect questionable conceptions of both childhood and learning in extreme claims such as "children must not be told anything, but must find out for themselves," and "children will learn to read in their own way and in their own good time."[13] Both of these claims imply a failure to recognize the relative brevity of childhood in the life span, and both suggest a teacher's role that skeptics find untenable.

The Role of the Teacher

Critics can object that the role assigned teachers in open education is in one sense too limited and in another too extensive and demanding. In relation to the latitude given children, the teacher's role is either too permissive or not positive enough. Yet the teacher carries too much responsibility if he is not guided by any predetermined set of intended learning outcomes sanctioned by his colleagues or a representative governing body. Such a responsibility could be safely entrusted to some teachers, though serious difficulties might arise even then in articulating their efforts with those of their colleagues. Teachers' wisdom is not so obviously outstanding, however, that society is prepared to let each one decide what to teach children. Even if a curriculum were provided, the instructional methods called for under open education would demand an extremely competent teacher. Any scheme that can only be carried out satisfactorily by geniuses is doomed to extremely limited application.

There is no question but that the teacher is the most important factor in most instructional situations. There is a question, however, as to whether the education of a child *should* depend so heavily on the competence of the teacher to whom he is assigned. Indeed, many efforts directed toward the development of instructional materials run counter to open education, in seeking to reduce rather than to increase the impact of the teacher.

"Education," according to Dearden, "implies processes of learning in which we come to understand and appreciate what is valuable in human life."[14] There are those who argue that there is no agreement on what is valuable, but Dearden believes that it is possible to identify a "quite substantial and acceptable consensus on what is basically valuable for personal and social competence in our form of life"—for being economically viable, for living with others in a justly ordered form of social life, for making worthwhile use of leisure, for the enjoyment of physical and mental health, and for valued forms of personal relationships. Teachers should not be expected to decide unaided what specific learnings contribute most to these values. Teachers have an exceptional degree of freedom in England and are "invited to be both philosopher-planners and men of action." This is an attractive thought, but not very practicable, as it requires teachers to "disperse their energies between defining the job and carrying it out."[15] Those who believe that individual teachers should not carry the responsibility for determining what should be learned in school will obviously be skeptical of any proposal that such decisions be left to young children.

In the matters of deciding which learning experiences children will have and of what direction to provide for them, open education is questioned on two grounds: first, for its neglect of systematic instruction and, second, for its disregard of the fact that no one method of teaching is best for all children, all subjects, or all teachers. There is evidence that for some kinds of learning, a given level of achievement can be attained in less time through the use of programed instructional materials than through other approaches. Although studies of "trait treatment interaction" have so far failed to identify which characteristics of learners interact with various instructional strategies, most experiments seeking to establish the overall superiority of a given method consistently show some children making greater learning gains with its competitor. Moreover, skeptics object not only to efforts to impose the open style and environment on all teachers and children, but also to the lack of balance in a child's school experience. One British headmaster has argued that happiness without achievement is no better than achievement without happiness, and that the primary school child should sometimes be noisy, sometimes quiet, sometimes move about, sometimes sit still, sometimes please himself, sometimes follow directions.[16]

Teachers can expect a skeptical response whenever they shun a positive role in which they function as authorities on the culture of a pluralistic society. If open education means that teachers refrain from setting high standards of achievement and conduct, from assigning tasks or giving directions, from providing systematic instruction based on accurate diagnoses, and from presenting information, developing understanding, or articulating values, then it will be rejected and resisted by many. Whether the teacher's role is permissive or positive, it remains critical and, hence, dangerous when it is not positive.

The Informal and the Amorphous

Despite the prevalence of a systems approach in the development of instructional materials, there is today a rather widespread distrust of the system, even among educators. As the instrument of the establishment, it is something one tries to beat or destroy if it seems unduly resistant to improvement from within. But system simply denotes planning and organization, demanding foresight and prudence. It implies order, structure, and form.

It is in this sense of form that education in schools is called formal education. Somehow the idea of formality has become associated with a kind of perfunctory conformity to meaningless, outdated conventions. Americans do not care much for formality; they prefer casualness. To be sure, schooling can become formalistic when learning proceeds in the absence of meaning and only form remains after substance has vanished. But in advocating informality in classroom relationships, one encounters a danger of rejecting form altogether so that informal becomes equivalent to amorphous.

In the arts, form is often of greater significance than content. Whatever relative importance form may have in education, it must be a matter of some consequence in curriculum and instruction, if not in management. In fact, the search for meaning, which is central to education, is essentially an effort to impose some form on phenomena and data to create some order out of what is initially chaotic and confusing. The conventions of symbol systems and of thought, which permit the acquisition of meaning, derive from the culture, not from the nature of the child. They are not acquired through discovery or the pursuit of spontaneous interests. In overemphasizing informality, whether in casualness of relationships, freedom of activity, indefiniteness of objectives, or improvisation of procedures, the proposals for open education appear to the skeptic to underestimate seriously the importance of both systematic learning and the learning of systems.

Much attention was directed at the nature of disciplines and the structure of knowledge during the decade of the sixties. While it may have been overemphasized, the systematization of acquired knowledge remains one of the chief benefits a child can derive from his formal schooling. Significant distinctions are often overlooked in informal, undirected experience, and many important relationships become discernible only after the imposition of a structure that is far from obvious.

The integration of all knowledge is a goal that has great appeal, but it is unlikely to result from an integrated day in which the various forms of knowledge to be integrated are not distinguished from each other. Merely permitting children to make choices without providing them a basis for choice is a disservice to them. What they need for autonomy are "systems of interconnected concepts and organizing principles" and "distinctive validation procedures for determining the truth, rightness, and adequacy of statements and judgments."[17] These are not discovered informally and spontaneously nor acquired as a by-product of good attitudes and general skills. They call for systematic, formal instruction.

The skeptic rejects the notion of self-expression without the counterpoint of discipline. "Self-expression is valuable only when the self is worth expressing," writes Dyson, adding that "no self can be fulfilled without being judged."[18] Standards, criticism, discipline, and restraint are advocated not to discourage or disparage self-expression, but to make it possible. As Froome puts it,

When children have mastered the basic fundamentals of written English and have begun to take pride in accurately written language, they will find, surprisingly, that ideas will flow more freely than before, because they will now have the skill to set their thoughts down in a form which others can take pleasure in reading.[19]

Activity as Means or End

In some of the material relating to open education, the skeptic finds the implication that all is well so long as children are in a wholesome environment and are engaged in certain kinds of activities. Thus, the activities seem to be treated as ends rather than means, just as some traditional teachers assumed that exposure to certain content was sufficient, regardless of whether anything was learned. But a learning experience entails activity directed at content for the purpose of attaining some specific learning outcome. There are many pleasurable and intrinsically worthwhile activities in which children might engage, but schools are maintained in large part to provide activities that are instrumental in bringing about desirable learning. Every self-selected activity is not likely to meet that criterion. Elaborate projects may produce impressive tangible results, but little or no significant learning. And as Crawford has noted, "discovery and project work ... to be done at all successfully, entail the trained ability to observe, read, understand, assess, summarize, and set out in clear systematic fashion whatever is discovered."[20]

There are occasions when it is valuable for children to discover things for themselves, but some learnings may never be discovered. While discovery learning is clearly less efficient than directed learning, there is no objective evidence that discovery results in better learning.[21] It is important to learn certain processes by performing them, but it does not follow that all subsequent learning should occur exclusively through those processes. If one has learned how to study independently, this does not mean he needs to learn everything independently. Similarly, a child can learn to work well in groups but still devote little time to group activities. Learning how to study is a valuable accomplishment, but there are many other valuable learnings to which newly acquired study skills can profitably be applied. The point is that no single kind of learning activity or teaching method is universally appropriate or inherently worthwhile. Professional judgment is probably a better guide to the instrumental value of an activity than is the inclination of a child.

Because children have a spontaneous inclination to play, it is often assumed that children learn best through playing. One can indeed learn from playing, but if the intention of an activity is to produce learning, then it is no longer play. The value of play is intrinsic, not instrumental. As Dewey noted many years ago, its anticipated result is not a specific change or production, but another subsequent activity. When play is used to achieve particular learnings, it is debased as the free and fluid activity it should be. Yet when it does not have learning as its desired end, play is simply recreational, not instructional. Children need to play and should play in school. But they also need to work and to learn the difference between play and work. The meaning and value of play would seem to depend in large measure on the contrast. When a person is permitted to do only what makes him happy, play loses all meaning. Play is debased both by becoming unrelieved and by becoming instrumental. The skeptic sees both possibilities in open education if self-chosen activity is treated as an end in itself.

A Skeptic's Conclusion

To the open education enthusiasts who say to their fellow teachers, "Be humane like us and give children autonomy in making their own choices, studying only what interests them, discovering things for themselves freely," the skeptic replies: "Be not so lacking in humility that you fancy yourself so much more humane than your colleagues that you should impose on them a teaching style that may be unsuitable both to them and to their children. Consider whether the primary school level is the one most in need of opening up, and whether the higher levels of education will be helped or hindered in doing so, if still greater openness is achieved at the lower ones. Consider, too, whether you base your practices on an overly-sentimentalized view of childhood and whether children might not be better served when their teachers play a more positive role, when their learning is more systematically structured, and when their experiences are varied in accordance with defined educational goals and diagnosed individual requirements." If the skeptic misconstrues open education, then advocates can disagree with him. But if his perceptions of open education are accurate, they can ponder his concerns with skepticism of their own.

2

Origins and Antecedents*

Joseph Leese

Cyclical patterns in nature are fairly well established. Season follows season as night follows day. The lemmings compulsively seek the sea while the salmon rush madly upstream to escape it. The patterns of social events are not so clear nor so well known, but it seems only a matter of time before the social sciences will have more knowledge by which to record and predict the nature of social events. Such knowledge may neither slow down nor speed up cyclical patterns, but it may provide a more reliable prediction upon which to plan and act. The certainty in the time prediction of the salmon run, for example, guides the plans and preparations for fishermen and canneries. Similarly, the history of hurricanes is the watchword of the West Indians to maintain their alertness in September and October.

The history of education is not exact enough to provide dependable guidelines to direct us in all our activities. Educational institutions, however, may have a cyclical pattern not dissimilar to those observed in the physical sciences. If such were the case, principals and teachers might better guide their actions in schools aware of some of the events likely to occur. If educational institutions were cyclical, there would be a useful basis for adaptation and redirection.

The enthusiasm with which a number of teachers, administrators, professors, and parents have seized upon the open school is disconcerting, since they are in large measure unaware of the historical antecedents of the innovation. Whether proponents of open education are simply rejecting or ignoring the past is unknown. It is clear, nonetheless, that many ardent supporters are quite uninformed about what has occurred previously, as solutions that have failed repeatedly in the past are proposed.

Criticizing the reform movement of the fifties and sixties, Silberman warns educators not to ignore the mistakes of the past as they attempt to relieve the crisis in education in the seventies.

The reformers by and large ignored the experiences of the past, and particularly of the reform movement of the 1920s and '30s. They were, therefore, unaware

---

*Assistance in the writing of this chapter was provided by James Rothwell, Senior Inspector, Primary Education, City of Manchester; Kathleen Langan, Director, the Parkside Experimental School; and Thomas Danson, Headmaster, St. Thomas of Canterbury Primary School.

of the fact that almost everything they said had been said before by Dewey, Whitehead, Bode, Rugg, etc. . . .

One result of this failure to study educational history, particularly the history of progressivism's successes and failures, was that the contemporary reformers *repeated one of the fundamental errors of the progressive movement.*[1] (My italics)

It would be a mistake to believe that Piaget, Hunt, Bruner, Holt, Kohl, and Weber have added nothing to educational thought. It would be equally unwise to believe that Dewey, Whitehead, Bode, and Rugg said nothing in the past that is relevant today. It is clear that educators should draw upon well-explicated theories and the successful and unsuccessful programs undertaken in the past.

It is encouraging to see that several books concerned with earlier educational reform have resurfaced.[2] These books identify main themes from the past, point out the origins of major proposals, and describe selected projects. They should be read by modern-day advocates of open education.

A Short History of
Child-Centered Schooling[3]

The need to reform schools and provide opportunities for the child to use his natural abilities and interests in becoming educated has a very long history. Rousseau, Comenius, and Froebel all recognized what Silberman has called "education for docility"—an intrusion upon the creativity and imagination of the child. The quotation he used from the *Great Didactic* written in 1632 is appropriate:

Teachers almost invariably take their pupils as they find them; they turn them, beat them, card them, comb them, drill them into certain forms, and expect them to become a finished and polished product; and if the result does not come up to their expectations (and I ask you how could it?) they are indignant, angry, and furious. And yet we are surprised that some shrink and recoil from such a system. Far more it is a matter that any one can endure it at all.[4]

Two centuries later, while visiting schools in Europe, Horace Mann found in Pestalozzian schools the reform needed to employ the self-paced reorganization of experience. In these schools, Mann reported that he never saw a child in tears because the teachers acted like parents—tender and vigilant. The schoolrooms were free of ridicule, invidious comparisons, and punitive redress.[5] Unfortunately, Mann suffered scathing rebuke from his colleagues in Massachusetts who appraised his ideas as nonsense—pandering to the child's gratification while inviting the abandonment of the obedience necessary to societal stability.

When the schools which Mann had established adopted the graded system, college presidents such as C.W. Eliot and William Rainey Harper decried this system because it demanded stereotyped individuals. By 1912, Frederick Burk, president of San Francisco State College, found the schools in a military malady that could do little else but destroy the interests of students to know and the urge to do. Burk asked, "Could any system be more stupid in its assumptions, more impossible in its conditions, and more juggernautic in its generation?"[6]

Dewey obviously had much to draw upon in his objection to the schools as places to insult children. Children were deprived of natural inclinations to learn and to develop through expanding play in the world about them. Dewey did not invent the idea of a child-aware school,[7] but he made a determined effort from 1896 to 1904 to bring to life what Mann advised educators in Massachusetts to do more than a half century before.

In *The Child and the Curriculum,*[8] written in 1902, Dewey summarized and postulated positions about the nature and growth of the child that Hall, the Gessells, Jersild, Almy, Piaget, and Erickson have been adding to since. In 1762, Rousseau said that the "most dangerous years in human life lie between birth and the age of twelve." Within that span, the central pervasive elements develop through which the individual becomes a self. It was a century later that Rousseau's assertion was supported by the empirical research studies reported by Bloom.[9]

Dewey knew what Dobinson claimed to be the most important Rousseau doctrine—that children must not be forced or motivated by threats to acquire organized structured knowledge. They must be given time to touch and test, watch and copy, discover and invent to create and extend meaning to their activities.[10]

In *Schools of Tomorrow*, Rousseau is paraphrased as follows:

"We know nothing of childhood, and with our mistaken notions of it the further we go in education the more we go astray. The wisest writers devote themselves to what a man ought to know without asking what a child is capable of learning." These sentences are typical of the "Emile" of Rousseau. He insists that existing education is bad because parents and teachers are always thinking of the accomplishments of adults, and that all reform depends upon centering attention upon the powers and weaknesses of children. Rousseau said, as well as did, many foolish things. But his insistence that education be based upon the native capacities of those to be taught and upon the need of studying children in order to discover what these native powers are, sounded the keynote of all modern efforts for educational progress. It meant that education is not something to be forced upon children and youth from without, but is the growth of capacities with which human beings are endowed at birth.[11]

The Deweys drew ideas from Rousseau that agreed with their own conviction—that the intuitive interests of the child should be genuinely cultivated and encouraged to gain access to the richest environment possible. They realized, moreover, that activity, if not directed toward some end, may result in developing muscular strength but have very little effect on the mental development of the child. The point is soon reached where intellectual discovery ends and mere repetitive performance of a task takes its place. At this point, teachers should see that children's intellectual growth continues while guiding them from impulsiveness.

Proponents of the British type of open education build their case on Dewey's ideas. They prefer, however, to draw from Piaget, although his inquiries are no more scientific. Indeed, sections of the Plowden Report read as if they were drawn directly from *The Child and the Curriculum.*

Play is the central activity in all nursery schools and in many infant schools. This sometimes leads to accusations that children are wasting their time in school: they should be "working." But this distinction between work and play is false, possibly throughout life, certainly in the primary school. Its essence lies in past notions of what is done in school hours (work) and what is done out of school (play). We know now that play—in the sense of "messing about" either with material objects or with other children, and of creating fantasies—is vital to children's learning and therefore vital in school. Adults who criticise teachers for allowing children to play are unaware that play is the principal means of learning in early childhood.[12]·

The above sentiments compare with the selections from Evelyn Dewey's comments over fifty years ago in reporting on Carolyn Pratt's New York City play school and on the Francis Parker School in Chicago.

Play is so spontaneous and inevitable that few educational writers have accorded to it in theory the place it held in practice, . . . Plato among the ancients and Froebel among the moderns are the two great exceptions. From both Rousseau and Pestalozzi, Froebel learned the principle of education as a natural development.[13]

Schools all over the country are at present making use of the child's instinct for play, by using organized games, toymaking, or other construction based on play motives as part of the regular curriculum. . . . The educational value of this play is obvious. It teaches the children about the world they live in. The more they play, the more elaborate becomes their paraphernalia.[14]

In the current wave of enthusiasm in the United States for a more relaxed and "humanistic" education, particularly in the early grades, there is evidence of American education sharing in the sentiments of Rousseau, Piaget, and Dewey. In responding to these sentiments, teachers are rejecting the theories of Jerome Bruner, who until recently saw salvation in a mere restructuring of cognitive subject matter.[15] Increasingly, the interests, feelings, and anxieties of children are uppermost in the minds of American elementary teachers. Thus, early childhood teachers began to reassert themselves in the mid-sixties.

The main ideas of Rousseau, Dewey, and the progressive-minded child educators, although rejected by many and deeply in the shadows for fifteen years after World War II, were never entirely eclipsed. Kept alive by those who did not run for cover at the hands of McCarthy, Rickover, or anyone else, they have remained as a bed of coals to provide a renewed warmth for children.

Part of the child-emphasis movement has been the widespread concern about people as individuals and the societal counter-effort to reduce the dehumanizing elements in a frantic, competitive, impersonal life. Another part has been the leadership of many school architects who believe that function follows form. The deluge of resource aids, films, television, and electronic devices has provided support. In addition, the importance of grades, diplomas, and certificates has been reduced as reflected in the increased demand to adopt academic standards for minority students and, indeed, all students. The most important factor that has gained the attention and conscience of those who work with children is the revived belief that children are persons and precious in themselves.

Educators should not make the mistakes of the wide-eyed progressives of the past, nor encourage uncritical spokesmen of open education. Instead, when possible, they should learn from the experience of those who have written and thought about children for the past three hundred years. To ignore the past is as ignorant as to reject a child's need for adult assistance and guidance.

Britain and the United States

Andreae is correct in her assertion, in Chapter 3, that it is absurd to believe that ways of learning and teaching that have evolved slowly over many years within one particular culture, can be transplanted and thrive unchanged in a totally different culture. She suggests, nonetheless, that Americans can learn much from the British. In this regard, I believe it is useful to distinguish some of the differences between the approaches used in Britain and those used in America.

First, teaching practices in British schools do not now depend solely on Dewey's digest and interpretation of ideas. They derive from a complex of interpretations from Froebel, Montessori, and Piaget, as reworked and restated in the Hadow Report,[16] and from the writings of Dorothy Gardner,[17] Nathan and Susan Isaacs,[18] and Ruth Griffiths.[19] In addition, teaching practices stem from the self-generation of many sensitive and devoted teachers who have learned from working with children that stimulation and response produce smiling faces, sparkling eyes, and deep and absorbing attention.[20]

Second, child-centered development has evolved at a slower and steadier pace in Britain than in America. Despite the past misuse of children in mines and factories, there has been an increasing tenderness toward children—not sentimental but warm, patient, and helpful. The war did much to augment this attitude when vast numbers of children were swept from their homes to be watched over, comforted, and aided by others while their parents devoted themselves to armament and defense.

Although educational provision was abandoned for the very young with the end of hostilities, it revived by 1955 to become a national pattern in Britain. In school at age three, most children are provided an atmosphere which caters to their naturalness, guides them in social maturing, and emphasizes the joy and pleasure of being in school. Gradually and without threat, they are moved from nursery to reception, to infant class, and to junior school. They are viewed as individuals and supported in their efforts to explore and acquire. There are teachers who are concerned that the pace should be accelerated but, generally, the pace is slow, tasks are self-generated, and adult presence is warm and reassuring while the child "stretches"[21] without threat. Children at age five amaze visitors from America with their ability to read, write, produce drawings, and pursue their work independently in classes where there are forty or more in classrooms, thirty-by-forty feet in dimension. The unperturbed, timeless guidance by the teacher leaves many an observer wondering how one can maintain such poise.

Third, British teachers generally have the same training and pre-service experience as American teachers. However, they come from and go into school settings where schooling depends more upon initiative than compliance; where exploration and cooperation are more important than competitive superiority; where support is more pronounced than imposition; and where supportive approval is more common than strict control.

Fourth, an important difference between the approach used in Britain and that in America has much to do with the degree of exploration allowed in schools. There is considerable freedom from curricular structure and specification in schools. The British pride themselves on the independence of the headmaster. Central administrative officers are consultants and guides. They make substantive decisions regarding buildings and finances, in-service education, projects and programs, but they do not tell school headmasters what to do, nor do they busy themselves with accountability paraphernalia with which to compare schools, teachers, and children. Headmasters, likewise, although immersed in the teaching of children, do not prescribe for teachers. Commercial materials and programed courses so often found in American schools are absent. It is true that programs such as those in the humanities, social studies, and moral education are now being produced by the Schools Council sponsored programs. Until recently all teachers had been on their own; thus, the teacher is guided more by what he believes to be best for children. His challenge to them is to try things out and to inquire on their own. Children often ask the teacher questions he cannot answer, so they explore together or seek assistance from others.

Most teachers have self-made exercises in mathematics, language, science, etc., and young children rather commonly work their way through such exercises within flexible time schedules. But the teachers, not the system, are master. The teacher's handbook, with its timed schedule and directions that so often serve to annoy teachers in America, appears to British teachers to be a condescension and an insult to their ability.

Behavioral objectives addicts now have their counterpart in Britain. They may in time increase in number and intrude upon the well-guarded independence of the primary teacher. There is little doubt that the encroachment will be slow. The freedom of children to respond, to adapt, and to choose from experience and wisdom is as much as anything that which Americans have dubbed "open." The British teacher, though, is suspicious of that label. She questions the so-called expert and the urgent drummer from the commercial publishing houses who offer their sophisticated wares. The British teacher senses that nothing substitutes for the warm and gentle, loving guidance of children from which grows a genuine thirst for knowledge.

Fifth, in this *loco parentis* position, the British teacher has always been secure in the understanding that his professional judgment about children exceeds that of parents. Parent-school groups are growing in Britain. This increased involvement of parents will likely result in increased parent questioning of educational programs, but responses will be given by confident British teachers and headmasters who are certain they know the type of schooling best for children. This constitutes another dimension of freedom and independence that leaves teachers to their own convictions, devices, and methods. Relieved of the meddling and threat of legislators and parents so common in America, British teachers have been able to get on with their job. This has given a widespread stability to their work and has increased the likelihood of experimentation and exploration while reducing the likelihood of cyclic outbursts.

The Future of Open Education

The current child-centered advocates in Britain may not be exactly like the child-aware enthusiasts who grew in number in America until the mid-thirties, but they have much in common. Open school proposals now in America are built on the same theories and convictions underlying the ill-fated progressive schools movement. The history of child-centered schooling has been markedly different in Britain and America. The future may be equally different. Will the present American enthusiasm for open education run the same course as progressive education? Will the British version simply follow a longer cycle than the progressive education movement in America?

The most troublesome question is why the current practice in British schools has evolved successfully over the same period of time in which progressive schools emerged and succumbed in America. The reason may be deeply implanted in the cultural differences between the British and Americans. While there are common characteristics, the British are more cautious than Americans. They are slower and more deliberate. It takes them longer, on the average, to make up their minds. They are less given to precipitant decisions followed by fretful efforts to make a thing work or come to pass. Consequently, they move along on a more extensively explored and more generally shared idea base.[22]

The Americans, by contrast, are impulsive and some view failure as a virtue. Historically, progressive schools were launched by a breed of persons given to adventure,[23] sustained by conversion as Cremin puts it. The schools did not emerge from a slow developing practice and a growing general conviction as did the British schools. Thus, as long as the energy and attention of the American initiator lasted, the reform efforts usually continued and survived. But when the generator of the program withdrew or retired, there was usually gradual retreat and abandonment. Some adventurers, of course, were summarily dismissed and successors were employed to return the schools to sanity and traditional ways.

The critics of progressive schools, defined more narrowly here as freer, child-aware, problem-centered institutions, see other reasons for decline. They contend that educational leaders were irresponsible; children's and the nation's futures were being tampered with; necessary and fundamental learnings were neglected; there was indefensible and injurious coddling; activity was frenetic and unproductive; parents did not understand, but when they did, they did not approve.

Americans certainly will not soon take over the cultural pattern of slow deliberation and muddling which gives the British some protection against a kind of cyclism. We may, however, employ some strategies that will help us extract a season of success if not guarantee an avoidance of regression.

A Successful Prototype

Ellsworth Collings' McDonald County, Missouri venture in 1923[24] is a good example of a successful "open" school that enjoyed considerable tenure. He fused many of the ideas currently found in the essays of Rogers' work, Weber's books, and the Plowden Report.

Collings drew heavily on the purposeful project method as explicated by Kilpatrick,[25] generally considered the most provocative of Dewey's disciples. He believed that the school should be a dynamic agent in an open community in which learning should predominate over teaching, where content should derive from the normal exposure of life, where active, productive involvement should characterize the process of education. He saw the essential goal of growth dependent upon increasing ability to discriminate, to relate cause and effect, to elect one course over another, to utilize all the intellective functions, and to generate balanced, creative interests.

Collings sought to enable children to be efficient in what they were actually doing and to be only secondarily interested in what effect the experience would have on future learning and life. He agreed that interests should grow naturally out of normal interactions of children with objects, each other, their families, and communities. Intrinsic interest was most important, not organized bodies of subject matter. Kilpatrick agreed that the child should first want to do something although it might be suggested to him by a teacher. He should manage his own inquiry or exploration. In the end, he should reflect upon and appraise his plans and procedures as well as his intentions. Out of this experience, the child should gain insight into how to make better choices and find the motivation to make more substantial inquiries in the future.

Collings employed four types of activities as structure: storytelling, construction, play, and excursions. As the child took interest, he was guided and supported but not directed or compared. When he lost focus, he was encouraged to explore why. What he needed or might explore was generally introduced by teachers with no thought to developing subject field competence.

The strength of Collings' project was that it was more carefully assessed than most other undertakings. Compared to traditional-type schools, the experimental group proved superior in achievement, attitude, and beyond school activities.

In reading Collings' reports, one can easily sense a replication in the projects of many elementary school programs. The difference is that most present elementary projects in American schools are well structured, thoroughly organized, and directed by the teacher. They are compressed into a period of some regular duration, surrounded and overpowered by the syllabus subject requirements, and permeated with external control and the competitive motif to which Rousseau and Dewey so vigorously objected. Under these circumstances, the project is neither a way of working with children, nor a vehicle for being present and patient while children explore and plan individually and in groups. It is not the instrument for unfolding and ripening as Kilpatrick wanted it to be. It is a mere concession and imposition forced upon children steered all too often by a strident, demanding taskmaster. Contemporary British teachers seem to be avoiding this compulsion to dominate and are more content to let the child develop his own ideas.

There are certainly other examples of schools in Britain and America now that compare favorably with Collings' school. But it is not seeing or mimicry that will produce "open" schools. Rather, it is a complex of ideas understood and acted upon as Kilpatrick said, "accepted to act on."

Backlash

Regardless of how hard teachers try to eliminate a backlash to open education, it is inevitable. There have always been traditionalists; there will always be traditionalists. More than that, it seems inevitable that every movement will have both its helpful and its destructive critics.

The authors of the *Black Papers*[26] in Britain represent backlash in its harshest form. They reiterate the claims made forty years ago in America by the essentialists, and a decade later by the basic educationists. In fact, one has but to read the blatantly slanted writings of several authors in the *Black Papers* to feel caught in a carbon copy of Bell, Lynd, Bestor, and others who sang the anthem in the fifties after progressive educators threw in the sponge.[27] Their hue and cry is not dead, although it is temporarily in eclipse. The recent study on reading by the National Foundation for Educational Research[28] is enough to keep the spark alive. In addition, the projected, more general inquiry on primary education practices may fan the coals into a bright light of exposure.

Reform movements have a way of fusing back into the mainstream, affecting it but not distinguishable from it. Proponents and supporters, and particularly copyists, tire of the new instrument that does not prove to be adequate for everything and especially not for the weakness they want corrected. Opponents lurking in the wings bide their time—waiting for a miscue to be used as the basis for a grand devastating entrance. A recurrent need emerges that requires a shift of emphasis. One powerful polemicist, such as Bestor or Rickover, intent on righting wrongs can, when the time is ripe, quickly assemble supporters and change the focus.

Yet, the worst enemies of reform are not critics so much as the panacea seekers who somehow believe that educational practice can be transformed over night by adopting a given innovation. Droves of Americans have descended upon British schools in the last three years. A good share of the visitors have as romanticized a vision about what they will see as when they rush off to "lighthouse" schools on visiting days at home. What they see, if they happen to like it, is really no more transportable from Britain than it is from Newton, Philadelphia, Dayton, or Sacramento. "Open" education, or any other kind of good education, has to be carefully and painfully nurtured through devotion and diligence if it is to withstand the rebuffs of critics. Brickell was correct when he said New York State teachers wanted most to see it happening before they would try it.[29] He did not, however, suggest in any way that if they liked "it" and if they tried "it," it would succeed.

If we are able to find teachers who can avoid sentimentalizing about children, know enough about knowledge to see its relationship to more esoteric knowledge, distinguish between organized effort and disorganized messing around, understand the complex growth process of children, we may forestall the cycling influences of cost, distrust, traditional value, and other directedness.

Conclusion

Our present interest in open education arises from a genuine discontent with what we are requiring children to do in schools. We have a conscience about stealing childhood from children. We are appalled by the conflict we seed among and within human beings. We are frustrated by the superficiality in the effort and product of the school's captives. We are ashamed of the revelations of child abuse in the name of education. We are annoyed at the irrelevance of the school and the failure of the disciplinists to make up for it through structure and syntax. We are intuitively repelled by the dehumanizers and efficiency cultists who want regimentation and external control.

There appears to be little doubt now that American schools will return to the methods and procedures that, as the British demonstrate, emphasize the child. Whether we will have the courage to leave him alone, to let childhood ripen in the child, as Rousseau put it, remains to be seen. The faith we have placed increasingly on Piaget's formulation may help us anticipate that assimilation upon which we must depend. The improved quality of our teachers may provide the enrichment and extrapolation we need for both balance and growth. Modern instrumentalists and organizational adaptation may supply the kind of support that brought success to the Dewey school.

There is always the danger, however, that like the salmon, we may exhaust ourselves in our effort. The behaviorists, led by Skinner, and the academicians, led by Bruner, constitute a powerful downstream current. It would be naive to believe otherwise. That the British infant teachers will slowly transform and refine the elementary approach in that nation is a foregone conclusion. But the behaviorists will not give them much support or leave them alone. Those who approve reform efforts here and in Britain have only an allotted time during which to stage their play.

The schools and the children are mere pawns in the power struggle between those who want self-direction and those who want to direct. In both camps there are those whose inclinations and appetites make them prey, in time, for their opposites. The wiser will always plead for the middle ground. They will seek a balance. They will warn well in advance about overenthusiasm, excess, misapplication, and overconfidence. They will call for restraint, caution, and review. The very proponents of the educational procedures Americans label "open" acknowledge the need for vigilance and prudence. Silberman has put it more bluntly: "One danger is that the American penchant for fads could lead to promotion of informal education as the panacea for all educational ills."[30] He goes on to say,

A certain continuing vigilance is also needed, for informal education can be as mindless in its own sweet, well-intentioned way as the arid formalism it replaces. Certainly there is a danger, evidenced in a few of the classrooms visited in England and the United States and perhaps inherent in the approach itself, that the pendulum of informality and child-centeredness may swing too far, thereby embracing the flabbiness and anti-intellectualism that characterized so many of the progressive schools of the 1920s, '30s, and '40s.[31]

Whether this occurs remains to be seen. But if the ebb and flow are inevitable, it would do educators well to extend their study of the past to ready themselves and children for the future.

3

Stages in Implementation

Jenny Andreae

As a person who was born in and has taught in Britain, I can testify that it does not make sense for a teacher to rush across the Atlantic for a package tour of a few besieged primary schools that are all too often in approximately the same stage of development as the school the teacher left. The British are very reluctant to recommend wholesale use of their method of education to others. Key authorities in Britain make this point quite clear, often to the disillusionment of visitors.

We can, of course, use a great deal of the thinking that has taken place in many schools in England. But the idea that ways of learning and teaching that have evolved slowly over many years within one particular culture can be transplanted and thrive unchanged in a totally different culture is absurd. In addition, the entire process is too often based upon a faulty assumption; namely, that open education is something that is already prepared so that one can use it instantly in his school or classroom.

Too often teachers have said to me after a Saturday morning workshop, "I'm going to open my classroom on Monday—you know, clear all the desks out, set up all the centers, and have the children choose what they want to do during the day." However many warnings I give, teachers find it difficult to realize that opening education is not a method that can be switched on and off, but a way of thinking and acting which reflects one's view about children. We are not dealing with a commercial program that can be demonstrated by a glib sales representative and adopted overnight. We are dealing with an evolutionary process which involves administrators, teachers, parents, and children.

An innovation cannot be instituted overnight, after a few days, or even after a one-week workshop. I am reminded of one school in a large city where nontenure teachers were instructed to engage in open education immediately. In one instance, a teacher's room was changed into centers while she and her class were at gym to ensure "it" happened! Open education has philosophical and pedagogical implications that defy its widespread and immediate implementation, even under optimal circumstances. Implementing opening education will be more widespread and effective if teachers and administrators are aware of the stages involved in attempting to utilize this highly complex concept. The purpose of this chapter is to discuss these stages of implementation.

Opening education needs to be defined before discussing the stages of its implementation. I use the term "opening education" or "opening a classroom" because I believe it is a more accurate term than open education or open classroom. If one looks up the word "opening" in the dictionary, two of the definitions are appropriate. One is a "planned series of moves"; the other, "acts or instances of becoming open." "Open" implies something that is complete or finalized, whereas "opening" implies growth.

Opening education in this country has the beginnings of a viable structure within which children can grow. The extent to which this growth takes place depends on the teachers' understanding of opening education. This understanding is based on the following premises, all of which are supported by Dewey[1] or Piaget:[2]

1. Children learn best when they have rich, first-hand experiences with concrete objects and situations.
2. The processes of thinking are action-based.
3. In a rich, stimulating environment, the child will discover, manipulate, plan, question, and practice those things that are important to him, although some children may at times need guidance and encouragement.
4. Materials should be appropriate to the child's level of thinking and be related to the child's acquired knowledge, experience, and interests. Thus, he may make a smooth transition from what is known to what is new.
5. By concentrating on what the child *can* do, the teacher is likely to gain the child's cooperation, confidence, and active involvement in his own learning.
6. The social context of the child's life is closely related to his cognitive growth; thus, continuing opportunities to talk, work, and share with children and teachers will enhance his cognitive growth.

It is possible for a teacher to share a commitment to these premises without necessarily being able to implement them. At this point, it is only necessary for the teacher to acknowledge that other persons can implement them and that he might also be able to do so at some future time. The degree of success that a teacher achieves will vary according to a variety of circumstances as well as to his personality. What is important is for the teacher to have the courage to take risks and, at times, to make mistakes. He should be able to accept criticism as well as to build on his experiences. He should also be able to cope with having many more questions than answers, and to deal with the inevitable frustration and depression that accompany change.

Implementation

In implementing opening education, one of the facts that becomes uncomfortably but increasingly clear is that the teacher determines its success or failure.

The amount of materials and equipment, the size of the room, and the facilities are not the most critical factors. More often than not, they are simply rationalizations for inactivity. What is important is the teachers' ability to use the resources available to the children's best advantage.

As there are teachers with different temperaments and personalities who attempt opening their classrooms, it follows that the processes and rates of change will be different also. An opening classroom is a more complex place than a traditional classroom. The mere fact that many different materials are used simultaneously calls for a drastic reorientation. Some persons are more adept at coping with complexity than others. For example, if a teacher is very orderly, the additional movement and noise in an opening classroom may worry him. If he finds detailed planning and organization difficult, then keeping on top of all activities in his room will probably cause him less difficulty. If a teacher strives to maintain control of the class because of the authority of his position, then allowing the children to contribute to their own control is going to be difficult for him.

If a teacher contemplates opening his classroom, he should ask himself some important questions: How much ambiguity can I stand? How did I react previously when I tried something new or different with my class? How much detailed planning suits me? In previous innovations, what worked for me and what did not? How a teacher responds to these queries goes a long way in determining the most effective way for him to begin opening his classroom.

During the past seven years of training and helping many teachers make the transition to opening classrooms, I have observed two main processes of change and growth. A majority of teachers I have observed and with whom I have worked belong to one or the other of two categories: "plungers" and "gradualists." It would be an oversimplification to suggest that there are no more than two such classifications. I have selected these two terms because of my empirical observations of teachers. Perhaps the stages I suggest will be developed further by researchers.

Both plungers and gradualists are able to reach their goals but at different times. While they often encounter similar problems, such problems do not occur simultaneously. The difference is that the plungers jump in quickly, are winded by the shock, pull themselves together, and follow up with a series of miniplunges which, in time, get them where they want to go. The gradualists, conversely, wait until the temperature of the water is exactly right and then move more smoothly and slowly.[3]

The Plungers

Stage One. Plungers consistently go in too deep and far too fast. They do not allow enough time for their children to work in a new way. They are then surprised and often disappointed that they cannot cope with the inevitable problems. Often, due to their lack of experience, they are not able to gauge the amount of time that children spend in an unfamiliar and perhaps chaotic setting. An example of this was in one district's summer school where the teachers set up lovely centers around their rooms,[4] only to find when the children arrived that this was only one condition necessary for learning to take place.

During this stage, the children are excited and very noisy, and there is the inevitable mess that results from more materials. The plunger finds he has to be able to think and do a hundred and one things at once. He wants the children to be independent and responsible, but some run wild and others become overly dependent upon him due, in part, to a lag in the development of their independence. This is not surprising when one considers how little opportunity children have to engage in independent activities in traditional settings.

If the plunger has any sense, he immediately retrenches, takes stock of the situation, attacks what he believes was the main cause of his problems, and tries again. This time, however, he proceeds more cautiously and carefully. Several problems then emerge. Children have too much material, too wide a choice of activities, and an unsatisfactory cleanup. It is now that the plunger begins to develop ways of coping with the overall situation. He often begins by limiting materials for the children to use and limiting the place in which to use them. He teaches children how to select materials and activities. He finds ways of keeping track of where children go, and he develops a plan whereby regular cleanup is accomplished by working together with children.

Stage Two. When the plunger realizes that he has, alas, only coped with surface problems, the second stage is reached. Now he begins to establish a regular part of the day in which children are able to function independently by using a variety of materials. He has found a place in the room for everything and has trained the children to replace materials in their proper places. But now several unexpected problems begin to disturb him. The children produce interesting things but always gravitate to certain areas of the room, such as the art area, woodwork, or blocks. No child goes near the book area after the teacher bans jumping on the couch and throwing pillows. No child wants to write, and few are interested in the mathematics area after having spent hours filling the scale pans a dozen times. The teacher believes all children should share something daily, but the sharing periods become unwieldy and even boring. But these are not the end of the problems. When does the teacher find time to display the children's work? What does the teacher do with all the things the children make? The room suddenly feels very cluttered and things disappear at the most crucial moment. As one teacher put it, "I feel as though the walls are going to move in on me at any moment," or as MacDonald and Zarat say, "You are locked in an open position."[5]

Gradually the teacher realizes his organization must change, so he goes through a period of constant furniture rearrangement. He begins putting away materials that are misused or unused and keeps out only a selected few. The room is usually so crammed with materials at this stage that children cannot focus or select. He begins to prepare children more thoroughly by telling them how long it is until cleanup time. He explains to them that he will look at a few interesting pieces of work with them, which he believes can be of value to the group.

Stage Three. This is perhaps the most frustrating stage of all. The teacher feels more on top of the situation due to his control of the children. He becomes aware, however, that he is accepting work that is sloppy and of poor quality. At first the teacher rationalizes this by saying it builds up the children's confidence. But it still concerns him that children are using materials in a repetitive way and are becoming bored. Academic skills are often not a part of the children's activities. Reading groups, phonetic drills, and mathematics worksheets are being crammed into one-half of the day. The teacher is very aware that other classes on the same grade level are on page 200, and his class is only on page 49. The teacher continually gets sidetracked. Record-keeping becomes a mammoth operation. There is not enough time to do everything.

The teacher gradually begins to realize that he is trying to juggle and succeed in two different directions and that neither, therefore, is succeeding. The children are aware of the differences and view one part of the day as play (when they experience enjoyment, interest, satisfaction, and involvement), and the other part as work (when the teacher sees them as bored and difficult to deal with). During the work time, they find it more difficult to listen and do what they now see as meaningless and irrelevant exercises.

The children's delineation of playtime and work time is the signal for another and more fundamental reappraisal. It is perhaps the biggest challenge that the plunger has to face because it constitutes a seeming philosophical contradiction. The teacher has consciously developed the children's skill of active participation, enlisted their cooperation and interest, found ways of making their experiences relevant, and encouraged their ideas and solutions to problems. The teacher realizes that during the activity time he has been a resource person, listener, and facilitator. But during the so-called basic skills part of the day, he has been a different person. What the teacher conveys to the children is that the academic work time is more important because this is when he becomes more authoritarian and pressured.

Stage Four. This stage requires a lot of courage. The teacher must decide that real learning *can* take place if he can provide appropriate situations and tasks. He must realize that he needs to strive for a balance for each child so that he can develop the necessary skills in all areas of growth. He must provide structures to support that growth so that many relationships can be established between so-called basic skills and other skills.

The Gradualists[6]

The gradualists proceed quite differently from the plungers. The following stages are those the gradualists are likely to experience:

Stage One. Unlike the plunger, the gradualist overprepares so that he can account for any emergency, real or imaginary. He selects a small group of reliable children who he feels can handle a new situation. He carefully instructs this elite group in how to use the materials and what to make with them. The activity is for a set time, perhaps as little as thirty minutes. The remainder of the class continues with regular work. As the teacher becomes more confident, he rotates the groups so that everyone in the class has a turn. However, the teacher gradually becomes aware that the activity is completely isolated and divorced from the regular work of the class. The teacher realizes that he is getting desperately short of ideas of what the children can do with the materials. One teacher I work with came to me and said in great distress, "I find I'm spending all my spare time trying to think of ideas that the children can use in the junk area. What can I do?" She had overlooked the richest source for ideas—her own children. I suggested that she discuss with the whole class some of the things they could make with certain pieces of junk, thereby enlisting their contribution and widening the possibilities. Or, she could introduce a broad topic for the children to interpret in their own way.

As the children become more experienced in handling materials, the teacher needs to deal with more detail so that he uses materials more successfully; for example, how to make handles on clay pots or how to cut out a pattern. All this adds up to a nagging feeling that the children could be doing more by extending their projects. When this happens, the gradualist moves on to another stage.

Stage Two. At this stage, the gradualist makes time more flexible for the children to do different kinds of work. To accomplish this, some teachers use what they call a "contract system" which, in fact, is an assignment system. To be a true contract, both parties involved are in mutual agreement; whereas, an "assignment" is a unilateral decision on the part of the teacher. In the latter, children are expected to fulfill daily requirements in the academic areas and in an area of their choice. They may choose when and in what order they do their assignments. From daily assignments the contract is extended and becomes weekly assignments, with an extensive weekly conference with the teacher to check what has been done and to plan what needs to be done next in all assigned areas. Each child usually has a large folder bulging with enough ditto sheets in every area to last a week. This seems to be the ideal arrangement for awhile, as all the children are accounted for in academic terms and are working at their particular level and rate. In addition, they are able to use materials and make things they choose to make. After a while, however, the teacher notices that ninety percent of his time is now spent searching for all the necessary dittos at every level. Also, during the day he is caught "in a corner" having endless conferences with individual children. As one teacher remarked to me at this stage, "What do I do about group and class teaching? I feel I should still be working some with groups, but there is no time now."

Somehow the teacher is no longer part of the mainstream of his room, but an overseer stationed at the sidelines. The assignment system, like any other system, works well for some children but is a disaster for those who spend the day drifting or daydreaming. No matter how many reminders from a teacher, some children have completed only a quarter of the work assigned. Others rush as fast as they can to complete all assignments and then the teacher does not know what to do with them. The teacher begins to see that most of the assignments are really "busy work" to make him and the children feel they are keeping up academically with the so-called requirements for their grade level. But the exciting links, the interrelatedness of projects and areas, are not happening. All the activities or projects children undertake are complete and yet they earn nothing other than a check mark on their weekly assignment sheet. After all the teacher's effort, he has, in fact, only trained children to reach the goal of filling out neatly categorized areas each week on an individual chart. Regretfully, the teacher realizes that the children are not satisfied with this accomplishment. They comprehend the exercises but, put simply, they only learn the skill of filling out a ditto sheet. As the teacher begins to realize these limitations, he moves onto the next stage of growth.

Stage Three. At this stage, the teacher sees more clearly that he has to provide much more input into the learning activities of the children to develop and extend those emerging individual and collective interests. In the teacher's search for individualization he has, paradoxically, become "locked in isolation" as have the children and the curriculum. It is perhaps more difficult to move out of this stage for the gradualist than for the plunger. He needs to find ways of integrating the children's day. One way of working toward this is to begin to foster more collaborative efforts with the children, let them work together and help each other on different projects.

Coordination

Gradualists and plungers work normally in self-contained or modified self-contained classrooms. If a gradualist and a plunger coordinate their efforts by working together, a plunger may gain the strength of discipline of the gradualist and, conversely, the gradualist may gain from the plunger's confidence in taking risks. The gradualist has the strength of individualizing, while the plunger has the strength of dealing with complex situations.

Whether a gradualist or a plunger, the important point is to know there are stages of development. If teachers are conscious of the stages, their chances for success are enhanced. Within the stages, teachers will develop checkpoints.

Key areas for both gradualists and plungers to concentrate on are as follows: (1) How should the teacher expand and develop the children's questions and interests? (2) When is it useful to intervene and when should the children be left alone? (3) How can the teacher develop the intrinsic potential of different materials and situations? (4) How may the teacher observe children more effectively?

I have noticed that gradualists and plungers begin to develop a system of rules for themselves and collect a conscious repertoire of strategies that are based in part on their knowledge and experiences with children. They learn to have greater trust in their power of intuition. They have less need for the popular segmented sequential steps and precise prescriptions. Intuition is an essential part of being a teacher. Without it, all the resources and techniques will fail. Gradualists and plungers must first cope with the feelings of guilt and anxiety that come when they break away from what is accepted and known. They must allow for these feelings as they are part of the process of change and growth. They arise from the previous unquestioned dependence on the traditional "system."

Most persons suffer from an impatience and a need for instant gratification and success. This is a reflection of the society in which we live. An understanding and awareness of this fact helps to give us patience as we search for results. All of us have moments of doubt and panic that children are not learning in an opening situation. This is partly because it appears more difficult to detect, and often we do not trust what we see. Our observations become limited so we revert to judging growth in previously accepted academic terms. In the process, we see only the tip of the iceberg. In opening classrooms, the teacher cannot reassure himself on a daily basis that children are getting the information he wants them to learn which the conventional workbooks, dittos, and quick tests so conveniently conveyed. Instead, he has to look deeper for instances that show where growth is taking place. This is difficult as growth is never made on a continuous course.

With an increasing repertoire of skills and internal awareness, the teacher learns to specify the kinds of assistance he needs. He does not rush off to every speech and conference on open education. He tends to be more selective in searching for consultant help. He talks to fellow teachers and begins to read journal articles and criticisms rather than strictly narrative accounts of teachers' experiences. He tries to gain more time to develop his intellectual and aesthetic resources. In this way he renews himself and the children with fresh ideas and resources.

The process of opening a classroom is not easy. The teacher will probably experience much discomfort and frustration as the situation changes. Eventually, however, the earlier struggles will begin to bear fruit. The gradualist at stage four is hardly able to believe he created such an overstructured environment in his earlier stages. The plunger at stage three will be similarly dismayed at his naiveness regarding children at stage one and his overresponse to problems in stage two.

Opening education requires teachers who are not only competent in teaching basic skills and interrelating them to all areas of the curriculum, but who are also able to plan for and structure situations so that the children can have considerable freedom in their choice of activities. It requires teachers who are able to recognize problems and who have the ability to step back and analyze what caused these problems. In this way, the teacher and the children will experience the delights of creative learning.

The Opening of an Open School

Lilian Myers

The day finally arrived. Five mothers and three fathers stood in the warm September sun with their combined total of sixteen children waiting, watching, listening. One of the parents looked up and shouted, "Here it comes, here it comes!" There was much scurrying of big and little feet, getting the children slightly calmed down and ready to go. As the bus pulled away with all its noisy passengers, one could see and hear the tumultuous cheering, pattings on the back, huggings all around, and shouts from the parents, "We did it! God-damn-it, we did it! We got the bus, and we've opened the school!"

This group of parents was among those who had pressured the district's board of education to establish an open education school. The struggle had been long and tedious. Little did they know, as they stood congratulating each other, that their exuberance would be short lived. For some, it ended when they talked with their children after school that same day. For others, it ended when they visited the school during the first week.

Introduction

Open education has been discussed, advocated, and variously implemented since the British primary schools were brought to the attention of the American public in the late sixties. Without understanding the principles on which the schools are based, without adequate parent and staff preparation,[1] without a knowledge of curriculum and curriculum development, and without agreement on roles for administrators, teachers, and parents, the open school may well become the Edsel of American education.

This chapter reports the findings and analysis of observations concerning the opening of an open school. Its focus is the curriculum development process, a major area of confusion in open education. Indeed, many proponents of open education maintain that curriculum as a field of study does not exist and that each child is the embodiment of a curriculum. Others maintain that any curriculum with a priori objectives is antithetical to open education.[2] Without doubt, every school has a curriculum whether it is formal or not. Those who ignore this fact, do so at their own peril.

In emulating the British primary schools, the open school will have a structure. It will have a curriculum, i.e., "a structured series of intended learning outcomes."[3] Using Johnson's definition of curriculum as a point of departure, I sought the answers to the following questions: (1) What is the curriculum of the school? (2) From what sources do teachers select components of the curriculum? (3) What selection criteria are used by teachers? (4) Who is involved in curricular decisions? In addition, I sought to determine the factors that cause teachers to impose institutional rules and procedures in an open school.

Data for this chapter were obtained from tape-recorded sessions of staff meetings held every Wednesday afternoon. Responses to the five focal questions were elicited from these recordings. Structured interviews were held with teachers and teacher aides on an individual basis to enlarge upon data not covered in the staff meetings. A questionnaire concerning the curriculum was sent to all staff members on a biweekly basis. A general questionnaire covering items such as years of teaching, number of children in class, grades taught, etc., was also sent to all staff members. There was an 86 percent response on both questionnaires. Visits were made to all classrooms, and observations relative to the report were recorded on tape. Access to all information on the school was obtained from a parent and a teacher.[4]

Background

The school is located in central New York in a city with a population of approximately 75,000. The socioeconomic level of the attendance area of the school is made up of persons in the upper-lower and lower-middle classes. The school opened in September, 1972, largely through the efforts of 37 sets of parents in the community in cooperation with the board of education and superintendent of schools.

The parents in the community and one teacher spent a year in planning before submitting their proposal for an open school to the board and superintendent. The mandate to "establish an open school" came from the board of education, whereas the "institutional plan" (the objectives of the school and how they were to be carried out)[5] was the responsibility of the parents. At that time, the parents decided to leave the curriculum planning and development to the teachers, as they thought teachers more qualified to handle this aspect of the program.

Before the staff was hired, the parents had decided to interview only those who were familiar with or had taught in an open school. There was a scarcity of persons in the area with those qualifications. The proposal for the school was approved in late July, and since the school would be opened in September, the parents had to select those persons who seemed the most promising. Three teachers, five teacher aides, and two specialists (art and music) were hired in August. One teacher was hired three days before the school opened. This teacher was a proponent of Neill's philosophy for Summerhill.

Of the four teachers hired, one had one year's experience with kindergarten children and was responsible for first and second graders in the school. Another teacher had one year's experience in a junior high school and was responsible for two groups of kindergarten children. A third teacher had several years of experience in an elementary school and was hired by the administration specifically to teach the older children in the school. The fourth teacher had experience in a free school and a junior high school and was responsible for third and fourth graders. One teacher aide had several years of experience in an open school (an excellent teacher who resigned in the third month ostensibly for health reasons) and was responsible for the art classes. Another aide had several years of experience in a junior high school, and the other five aides had less than two years of teaching experience or none at all.

. Most of the staff (teachers and aides) met daily from 9:30 until 5:00 for three and one-half weeks before the school opened. During these sessions, the conversations centered around the philosophy of the school, materials and supplies to be used, decisions on who would be responsible for which group of children, and the setup of the classrooms. At this time, the staff assumed that materials and supplies were to be purchased with the funds allotted them by the board of education. These funds were late in materializing. Kindergarten supplies were brought in from other schools. The library was stocked through the efforts of a state department official who was able to secure free books from a publishing company. The books covered many different topics and were all published within the past two years.

No one reviewed or selected any of the books that were placed in the school library. There were quite a few picture books that could be used by the younger children, but as one teacher aide said, "Sure there are some nice picture books for the kindergarteners, but most of them, and you can pick out any one from any shelf, are geared to the junior and senior high school level. They are literally useless in this school."

The school opened with an enrollment of 120 children from the ages of five to eleven. Exclusive of facilities, teacher salaries, and utilities, the board of education allocated $10,500 to the school for instructional materials and supplies. The site of the school was a building used previously as an elementary school but which now housed offices in the upper floors of the building. The school occupied the first floor and the basement of the building. Fourteen rooms were used for the school including an auditorium, library, gymnasium, and various rooms converted into shops, art rooms, dark rooms, and the like.

In attempting to establish an open school fashioned after the British primary schools, it would seem that parents who supported the idea and teachers who were to implement it would be fairly knowledgeable in the area. Both groups, however, were only vaguely familiar with the British primary schools. Two of the staff members had seen a filmstrip on the schools and had read a few articles and books by authors such as Kozol, Neill, Holt, and Goodman. Some of the parents too had read material by these same authors, but few of either group were familiar with works such as those by Rogers, Brown and Precious, Barth and Rathbone, and the Plowden Report.[6]

The situation was not unlike setting out from England for the New World, knowing in which general direction it lay, making copious observations along the way, but waiting until reaching mid-ocean before determining the course and the nature of the vessels.[7]

The Report

1. What is the Curriculum of the School?

When the first question was asked of the staff after the first week of the school's operation, one teacher aide commented:

When the school opened, we planned to do what the children were interested in: games at first to just enjoy themselves, some art material; and we encouraged them to write stories. We had lots of gym time, art and music. We also had lots of chaos. It was very confusing. I was really worried at what was going on—nothing much.

The sentiments expressed were indicative of all staff members' responses to the question. One teacher said, "We don't have any curriculum at all." Oddly enough, teachers seemed compelled to begin without limits and work toward them rather than the other way around. Such a tendency defies learning theory and general psychology.

There was unanimous agreement among the staff that the first week was chaotic. Rather than focusing on a curriculum, the staff found itself concerned mainly with order, discipline, and noise level as well as keeping track of children and getting them interested in the limited number of supplies and materials.

At the first interview of individual staff members, I asked what curriculum was decided upon during the August planning sessions. All of the answers were the same—there was no written curriculum decided upon before the school opened. The following comments from the staff are representative of the atmosphere and outcome of the planning sessions:

There were no formal written statements of objectives or curriculum before the school opened. We selected certain written objectives from other schools and mentally made a list of our own. Nothing was written down.

We talked a little about my duties, but since no one else knew how to conduct an art course, they said I could do whatever I wanted to do. I have a few years' experience in teaching art and have my own ideas, so they have worked out pretty well.

During those meetings in August, what we did mostly was move furniture around. Very little of that time could be used for planning. I kept wanting to talk about what specifically we were going to do with the children, but the discussions we had centered around the general philosophy of the school.

We didn't set up a basic skills program. We didn't feel the need to. We all assumed and felt too that the kids would get all the basic skills they needed from their activities—art, science, shop, gym, paper airplanes, and music. This was our curriculum.

When the planning sessions ended prior to the opening of the school, the following items had been decided upon concerning the curriculum: (1) Teachers would be responsible for ordering their own curriculum materials. (2) Teachers would be responsible for the curriculum in their own classrooms and for their own students. (3) Teachers would guide the teacher aides in the curriculum and offer suggestions to other teachers on those techniques or materials that were useful in their own classrooms.

Since there was no formal written curriculum, and since the teachers decided initially to be responsible for the curriculum in their own classrooms, the first question is not easily answered. The very nature of this open school makes it necessary to describe the staff's "curriculum development process."

Much to the consternation of the staff, the first week was chaotic. By the second week, the atmosphere had calmed down enough to inject the following activities: drawing, playing with blocks, listening to music, painting, working in the shop, and listening to stories. In the next few weeks, other activities had been included such as modern dance, filmstrips, Spanish, scale work, and others. The major change in the first three weeks, however, was the formal inclusion of academic skills in the "curriculum"—reading, writing, and mathematics. Complaints had been made in the second week that the school was not academic enough to satisfy many of the parents. I asked the staff members' impressions of this change. Some of their comments were,

I do have more of the three Rs now. I didn't have any in the beginning because I was just learning or seeing how I might conduct the class. Some of the parents have asked us to spend more time on the three Rs. I don't mind, it gives the kids more things to do.

The program has become more rigid because the children were wandering around not knowing what to do. The parents were breathing down our necks and wanted us to get some basic learning going. After two or three weeks, I had to structure the class more.

My course requires children to come in regularly so that they don't lose what they have learned. Since I am now getting the small children at definite times and days, it has become easier to work with them on certain projects. In this way, the curriculum has become more rigid, but it is a good thing.

By the end of September and throughout October, classes became even more structured with the inclusion of the three Rs, grouping the children, and the use of workbooks and worksheets. Within this period, the staff was still very concerned about the children's behavior in the classroom, respecting each other and the materials, giving them a sense of security in the school, teaching them to adhere to specific school restrictions, and trying to instill in them a sense of responsibility for their own learning.

When the school opened, there was no formal curriculum. During the next few weeks, the three Rs became more prominent. By November, the classes were highly structured—the children were grouped, the three Rs were compulsory, there were daily assignments, and there was less free time and more busy work.

One teacher, upon reflecting on this change, advanced the "philosophy" of the school:

Our philosophy is the assumption that all children will want to learn if you create an environment that is exciting for them and that they will learn much more quickly at their own individual pace and with their own individual interests than they will in a structured group. We wanted this school to be oriented to the individual child. If you do things that interest him, that turn him on, that excite him, he will learn much more than if you forced him to sit down in a group and do pages 4 or 5. And I still believe that, but it's not working here.

In spite of the change, one teacher ended an interview on a positive note,

We didn't have enough time to develop a good curriculum. We more or less threw things together. We plan to have a workshop in curriculum next summer for our next year in the open school.

The above statement is representative of Smith and Keith's discussion of the "true believer" phenomenon. "From the doctrine and facade, comes the motivation to carry on beyond what real, day-to-day results seem to justify."[8] Because of their belief in the doctrine of the school, most of the staff maintained a positive attitude despite the growing opposition to their educational program from the parents and the administration.

The teachers viewed curriculum as all the experiences children have in school. This definition, while widely accepted, excludes nothing and is, therefore, hardly a definition. The teachers had planned to have a learner-centered curriculum where children could select their own activities. They had planned to guide and direct the children into activities that would be useful to them. They had planned to teach children to be responsible for their own learning. They had planned to show children what a joy freedom in learning could be. They had planned to work as a cohesive unit without a principal or headmaster with these objectives in mind. Above all, they were dedicated to the idea that children will become responsible for their own learning in an open atmosphere, free from the restrictions in the usual traditional school. Unfortunately, what the staff had planned, or more accurately thought, did not materialize.

In November, I asked the teachers if sufficient time was allotted by the staff to plan together new curricula. With the exception of the two specialists, most of the answers were similar.

We do not have enough time to develop a good curriculum.

We don't have a regular meeting schedule, but sometimes the two of us will talk about thirty minutes after school about things that have worked in our own classrooms. There isn't a lot of planning on specific things we will do in the classroom.

I do talk with the other teachers if I need help, but they don't really suggest anything. I'm supposed to do as I see fit.

I don't have twenty-four hours a day to spend on this job.

In short, there was minimal planning and much compromising. The teachers were pressed into compromises and selected what they thought was best.

2. From What Sources Do Teachers Select Components of the Curriculum?

During the planning sessions, the teachers had sought to formulate a philosophy on which to base their educational objectives and, from these, to derive a curriculum. The philosophy developed was not comprehensive even though, as will be indicated later in this chapter, philosophy was the major topic during most staff meetings. The teachers' views on philosophy centered around ideas from a kit on open education,[9] readings by Neill, Kozol, Maslow, Rogers, et al., and their own knowledge about children. Based upon this "philosophy," the sources used in selecting components of the curriculum were the children and an idealized contemporary society.

Two weeks after the school opened, because of the constant haranguing from parents and administrators, the staff began to select curriculum materials out of desperation. They saw something that looked useful in educational catalogs or asked teachers from other schools what to use. They included any and all materials that were brought in from the community, from other schools, by anonymous donors, and by themselves. Some of the reasons for these selections were "the children think it's fun"; "the readers and workbooks are open-ended, so that the children can work by themselves"; "we have so few things to work with that anything will have to do."

As noted, the school did not have a curriculum, at least as defined by authorities in the field.[10] The "curriculum" that existed, nonetheless, evolved from a variety of sources or, perhaps more accurately, forces. Due to the small amount of funding, which was not readily available for a number of reasons, the materials and supplies were brought in from other schools, the community, and teachers themselves. The staff had no recourse but to use these materials to the best possible advantage in working with their curriculum. Thus, the curriculum was selected as a result of the resources available in the school.

At the outset, the staff quite often had to search for supplies or had the parent scrounge committee canvass the community and other schools for needed materials. In addition, the staff was inexperienced in the selection of curriculum materials by which to achieve their anticipated objectives. The fact that parents demanded additional academic work later in the school year required additional resources. The resource limits in the open school seriously endangered the life of the school. This observation supports Smith and Keith's hypothesis that "the phenomenon of beginning an organization, and especially an innovative organization, requires more resources than usual, and second, that the unanticipated consequences of each purposive social action will require an added increment of resources."[11] In this instance, funds for additional resources were not readily available to the staff and, thus, the conflict between parents' demands and teachers' lack of resources seriously hampered the life of the school.

The administration, as one teacher put it, "out there somewhere," also played a large part in the selection of components of the curriculum to correspond with the open school facade[12]—the manner in which the school was presented to the public. Some children, for example, were directed into specific activities for the benefit of the numerous visitors to the school and for the television audience. The school had gained much attention from the outlying areas because of its new venture into open education. Thus, the administration as well as parents sought to maintain the open school facade to the public in spite of any and all problems.

3. What Selection Criteria Are Used by Teachers?

The criterion used in determining the selection of curriculum was essentially conventional wisdom. Various activities were selected "to instill self-responsibility in the children for their own learning"; "to learn to cooperate in creating a large project"; "to see that by working together they can accomplish a great deal." Not all of the reasons were positive, however; some included the following:

It's becoming unbearable for those children who settle down to something constructive and for their teachers or aides to function properly in this sort of surrounding. The workbooks keep them busy.

We have not been able to communicate a feeling of the learning process to the children. It is hoped that with proper orientation of these new materials, this feeling will come across.

The children would be able to work at their own speed and the readers were predicted to be workable which is good because there is a lack of organization in the classroom. It is useful learning and it is busy work.

In addition, the staff was under pressure from parents, administrators, and the board of education to restrict the movement of some children to lessen the chaos. The Nuffield readers and all of the workbooks selected were open-ended. The staff worked with those items that would keep some children busy, rather than with what the children needed or lacked. One teacher said he used the workbooks to "give me space to develop a really rich curriculum in the open school sense."

Some members of the staff selected materials based on their past experience in using them. They had been successful in allowing children to learn on their own with these materials. Other materials were recommended by teachers from other schools. In addition, many materials were selected from educational catalogs. These items were selected on the basis of the amount of enjoyment children might get from them, the selling quality of the advertisement, and their visual presentation in the catalogs.

The music teacher used equipment of his own or purchased items himself. Some of the literature used in his course had been purchased through the librarian because the present library was inadequate for his purposes. Most of the equipment used in his course was made by himself and his students.

One teacher aide made the following comments about the materials she used in her classroom:

I worked with the books I am now using when I was practice teaching. I didn't know what first graders should be learning. I got these books from a school that had extra copies and wasn't using them. There were some books sitting in David's classroom, and he told me to go ahead and use them, so I did. Today, the Macmillan series arrived, so I will be using them also. With these books, the children can work on their own. At one time, I was desperate for materials, so I used the linguistic books, which I think are dreadful but the kids don't mind them and they are learning from them; so I still let them use the books.

These comments were made on November 12, two months after the school opened. Thus, no rational system existed for the selection of the curriculum. Rather it was more an example of get what you can from whatever source or resources available.

4. Who Is Involved in Curricular Decisions?

The staff decided initially the curriculum that would be useful when the school opened. They were in accord that "the parents had nothing to do with the curriculum." The teachers had planned not only the specific activities within their own classrooms, but also to give the children various choices within those activities. Although the activities were designed to include the basic skills of reading, writing, and mathematics most of the staff did not know how to combine these skills with the activities.

A week had barely passed when pressure for emphasis on the three Rs came from parents. Shortly after this, more pressure came from the administration and board of education. Thus, within a short span of time, the desires of parents became the demands made upon the teachers. The inclusion of the three Rs by the administration in a formal dictate, was received with mixed emotions from the staff. To some, it was seen as interference from laymen and a threat to their authority; to others, it was a godsend. In spite of the formal inclusion of the basic skills, the staff continued to maintain that they made all the curricular decisions in the school.

For the first four weeks, the staff met regularly at the school every Wednesday afternoon from 12:30 until 5:00 (children were dismissed at 12:15). At these meetings, the staff anticipated discussing individual children and the total educational program. When the meetings began in September, parents, administrators, observers, and other interested persons attended and many brought up their problems to be discussed with the staff. The teachers were barraged from all sides with questions, grievances, and complaints by most of those attending. By the time everyone else's problems were aired, the staff had only about an hour to discuss their own problems among themselves.

By the sixth week, the staff decided to leave the school as soon as the children were dismissed at 12:15 on Wednesdays. They went out for lunch, had a cocktail or two, and as one staff member put it, "We were then able to face the firing line in a more relaxed mood." After a couple of weeks, the strain between the teachers and parent group increased, and future meetings were held at the teachers' homes without the parents (or the parents were asked to leave after one hour), but with two administrators and myself. Even in these meetings, the atmosphere was much the same as before. Discussions centered mainly around discipline and order in the school, curriculum material selection from catalogs, the purchasing of supplies, and the philosophy of the school. More time, however, was spent discussing individual children than had been the case in previous meetings.

One administrator's contribution to the meetings was a regular discussion of administrative procedures, rules and regulations, and the ordering of supplies. He was originally thought of as a possible candidate for principal of the school but rejected by the parent group. Most of the teachers and aides resisted his being appointed principal, as his overall conception of the school was in direct contrast to their own views of how the school should operate. In effect, if he were hired as principal, the teachers' authority in the total educational program would be reduced significantly. As Orlosky and Smith pointed out in their study on educational change, "Changes will be resisted if they require educational personnel to relinquish power or if they cast doubt on educator roles."[13] There were no other candidates for the position and no recruitment of any at this time.

By the second month, the school was in such a state of disorganization that the parents suggested to the staff that this same administrator be appointed as principal. The implication was that the central administration recommended that a principal be hired. The administrator's earlier "weakness" of being too structured was suddenly viewed as an asset to the operation of the school.

Before school began, parents and teachers made much of the idea that the school did not need a principal. Unwittingly, however, they demonstrated dramatically just the opposite. Barth concludes that "There must be a person on hand under the roof who can assess needs and match appropriate people and money to them."[14]

Since the school was mandated to be an open school, the central administration allowed the parents and staff initially to be totally responsible for the school's organization and educational program. However, with the onslaught of complaints from parents and the community, the administration tightened its grip on the school and demanded more control over children and more academic work. The growth and formalization[15] of the school was facilitated when a principal from the school district was hired at the end of January. The parents and administration felt that the floundering of the staff was much too detrimental to the children in the school, the reputation of the district, and the integrity of the parents.

5. What Factors Cause Teachers to Impose Institutional Rules and Procedures in an Open School?

Before the school opened, the staff decided not to have any written rules for the children when they arrived. This would have been contrary to their "philosophy" of an open school.

We didn't see having a list of rules for the children the first day or even week because it was their school and they might have felt that it was just another traditional school with a new name.

There were several general rules that were more or less understood by teachers. For example, children were not supposed to hurt anyone else, infringe upon each other's rights, or destroy each other's property. All other rules were to be made on an ad hoc basis.

The first week was total bedlam. Teachers, aides, and volunteers were literally running around trying to find children; children were not signing in or out consistently in rooms or learning centers; children were mistreating each other; children were eating everywhere and at all times; children were climbing on window ledges, tables, stairs, and banisters. In effect, children were all over the place. One teacher said about the chaos, "This is not a school, it's a happening. We're beginning to employ King Kong tactics just to keep the kids in a classroom." Barth noted a similar situation in his case study of two elementary schools. The children took advantage of every privilege. The overriding priority was child control.

Children tested and abused every teacher who was attempting to run an unfamiliar classroom, until the teacher demanded conventional order or was run out and another came to take his place. Unless a traditional climate was provided, neither student nor teacher could find the classroom habitable.[16]

Teachers, aides, and volunteers were supposed to use their own judgment in dealing with unruly behavior, structuring activities, and directing bored or inactive children into various activities. None of this came about in the first week. Chaos reigned in the classrooms, in the halls, on the stairs, in the gym, in the auditorium, in the learning centers, and spilled out into the playground and onto the street. Every staff member was exhausted at the end of every day of the first week. One teacher said, "I went home and after going to bed, I couldn't sleep; I had nightmares every night. I said to myself, this can't be the open school we envisioned." Another teacher added, "I didn't have nightmares at night. On the contrary, the whole week was a nightmare. I really slept well at night; I was exhausted from the days."

By the third week, fourteen rules had been written, posted, and enforced rigorously. During the next few meetings, more rules had been added. On November 2, a notice was posted stating that no visitors would be allowed, except parents, until January 10.

Most of the staff said that the rules were enforced mainly for the safety of the children. A few staff members suggested that they were enforced because of pressure from the parents, administrators, and board of education. Still others claimed that rules were instituted and enforced "to preserve our sanity." It appears, in fact, that all of these contributed to the enforcement of rules.

Due to the lack of experience of most of the staff in dealing with children in this type of environment, institutional rules and procedures were necessary for their survival. Regardless of the staff's commitment to their philosophy of an open school, it was not enough to cope with the actual circumstances.

Altruistic intentions, impeccable academic credentials, abundant vigor, and unlimited educational vision will not, in themselves, suffice. As one of the custodians in the Program put it, "That and a dime will get you a cup of coffee."[17]

This particular open school supports Smith and Keith's generalization about a "protected subculture."[18] It had few of the organizational constraints of the larger school district. It made its own rules and regulations and planned its own educational program. It was essentially an autonomous school. Considering the inexperience of teachers in such a situation and the watchdog parents and administration, the genesis of formalization was rapid. The situation, as observed, also supports the hypothesis that "a new but autonomous organization moves through such a process of decisions, trial and error, activities, gradual growth, and formalization."[19] As the process evolved, one teacher commented during the third week, "Everything was going along fine before the school opened. We came in with late idealism, but now we're concerned with early survival."

The decision was made to open a school and, as a result of the teachers' trials and errors, more structured activities were gradually instituted. The hiring of a principal later in the school year contributed to the order and formalization of the school.

At the beginning there is hope, enthusiasm, and a sense of mission. It is not long before this invigorating climate begins to change, hopes dim, morale lowers, and the weight of tradition begins to extinguish the strength and capability of the desire to innovate.[20]

Conclusion

The development of a curriculum in this open school was not a rational process. It came as a shock to the teachers and aides involved. The dedication and commitment of the staff to the idea of the open school were not enough to ensure its success. In a sense, their strong commitment served as a detriment. Looking back on the situation, one teacher commented, "We wanted to turn the world upside down with this school, but we didn't realize that not many people could walk on the ceiling. We set out with the idea of giving children an educational feast, but we couldn't even provide them a snack."

None of the staff had been involved previously in planning the educational program of a school. They were swept along by their philosophy of an open school. Children were not involved in the planning, nor were they told explicitly what was expected of them in the school before it opened. How could they have been told? Even the parents and staff were unsure of the course they were trying to steer. The children had the idea that the school would be free and they could do as they pleased. The lack of communication among parents, staff, and children was inexcusable. One teacher said, "Where did the children get the idea that they could do anything they wanted here? Who told them? We certainly didn't." In fact, the children seemed incidental to the aspirations of parents and staff.

Although the parents were responsible initially for bringing the open school into the system, many of those who had children attending had no idea what actually would be going on in the school. For some, it was a place for their own problem children who had troubles in other schools; for others, it was conveniently located; for others, it was looked upon as a good school without the traditional approach; and for still others, it was seen as a desperate effort to deal with their own problems of living in a society which they felt helpless to control.

The teachers and aides in the school were unbelievably idealistic. They had not planned on having a child-dominated atmosphere; having to purchase their own materials and supplies after the school opened; the exuberance and spontaneity of children; having so few volunteers for assistance; the children's safety; the need for structured activities; having bored children; and how they were going to combine the three Rs with the children's activities. In short, as philosophical platitudes permeated the air, planning was virtually ignored.

The open school has five months left in the school year. The fate of one teacher (of the Summerhill method) is presently being decided upon by the administration. With the hiring of a principal, the administration has taken over much of the control of the school. One aide has been dismissed and two others hired. One specialist has resigned, and two aides have said they would not return the next year unless experienced open school teachers were hired. Volunteers are few and far between. Of 120 children enrolled, 86 remain. The other children have been withdrawn for a variety of reasons: the school is too free; the school is just another traditional school; the program is not academic enough; the school has too many problem children; there is not enough concern for children's safety; teachers are incompetent; there is a lack of materials and supplies; there is a lack of discipline; there is too much discipline.

Whether the school will survive the year as an "open school" is difficult to say at this time. The staff has become better organized and is spending more time than before on the curriculum and the educational program, not to mention the children. In spite of this, a tense atmosphere prevails throughout the school. Visitors will not be admitted until the middle of January. Because of the newness of the situation, teachers and aides felt they could not operate effectively with the children while visitors, concerned parents, and administrators were straggling in and out of the school at all times of the day. Winter vacation is approaching and the staff will then have an opportunity to reflect upon what has been happening in the school and to act accordingly.

This chapter was concerned with the opening of an open school and the implementation of a curriculum based on the philosophy of evangelists. Perhaps the analysis of the school is overly critical. I believe it is not. If a parent is considering placing his child in an open education school or a teacher is to be instrumental in starting such a school, both parties should be aware of some of the problems involved in such an undertaking. "American education can withstand no more failures, even in the name of reform or revolution."[21] Too many persons with "late idealism" are jumping on the bandwagon for open education without taking a critical look at its implications for parents, teachers, administrators, and most important, the students. It is only a matter of time whether this open school staff will have success in its endeavors or be party to the closing of an open school.

As a result of my observations, the following generalizations are offered concerning the establishment of an open school:

1. If a school has no institutional curriculum, i.e., a priori learning expectations for students that exist on paper or in the minds of teachers, the possibility of success for the school will be reduced.

2. The absence of an agreed upon definition of curriculum and the term open education will result in ideological quarrels leading to conflict or strain between various factions (within both the staff and parent groups) such as aristocrats vs. egalitarians, instrumentalists vs. pragmatists, or simply those who are viewed as permissive vs. those who are viewed as academicians.

3. A lack of agreement among teachers concerning sources for the curriculum will result in sources being determined by available instructional materials. The absence of an agreement regarding sources will result in a conflict or strain among teachers as to the most desirable source for objectives— students, academic subjects, the needs of society, or the anticipated needs of some future utopian society.

4. A lack of agreement among teachers concerning criteria for selecting instructional materials will result in criteria being determined by available instructional materials.

5. A lack of agreement about who determines the curriculum will often lead to conflict among the administration, parents, teachers, and students all of whom wish to maintain or increase their existing authority.

6. When institutional rules and procedures concerning student conduct are not explicit on paper or in the minds of teachers, children will seek to determine the limits of freedom that exist in the classroom and school, often resulting in a chaotic situation until teachers gain adequate control.

7. When teachers disagree about what constitutes desirable student conduct, conflict between teachers can occur and disorganization will result until some resolution is reached by consensus.

8. In a public school district, open schools that "slight" the three Rs can expect to come under immediate criticism, even from those who are sympathetic to the program of the school and who view themselves as liberal. In addition, open education schools that slight the three Rs will be forced to place more emphasis on these by administrators, parents, and even the teachers themselves.

9. If there is confusion as a result of disagreement concerning the curriculum, sources, criteria, lack of materials, or rules and procedures, teachers will create busy work for students as a means to maintain order. During this period, teachers may develop physical and mental illnesses resulting in absenteeism or even total withdrawal from the school.

10. If a board of education and central administrative staff agree, as a matter of policy, to permit open education to exist in a school as an experiment for a period of time and agree to assure it "autonomy," this policy will be terminated quickly if parent opposition results.

11. Teachers in open education schools who adopt the "alternative of grandeur,"

will tend to reject their educational program as unsuccessful and instead adopt a "facade of success." As in the Kensington study, "The organizational face presented to the public . . . did not reflect the reality of the school."[22]

12. Schools that begin without carefully developed means for attaining their goals will likely not achieve their goals.

13. Schools without a principal or a person acting in an administrative capacity will have difficulty acquiring materials and supplies, communicating with the central administration, coordinating the program, resolving staff conflicts, developing means for acquiring goals, and dealing with parents and the larger community.

5   **Status in New York State**

Donald A. Myers
Daniel L. Duke

During the 1971-72 school year, we visited 122 open classrooms in fifteen elementary schools. The fifteen schools were located throughout the State of New York[1] –from Long Island and New York City in the south, to Plattsburgh in the north, and Rochester in the west. Student enrollment ranged from 83 to 1,100. Six schools (two in New York City) were located in urban communities, five in suburban communities, and four in semirural communities. Students of six schools came predominantly from lower-middle socioeconomic class homes; five schools served children from predominantly middle socioeconomic class homes; and the enrollment of four schools came from middle and upper-middle socioeconomic class homes.

Methodology

The first problem we encountered was securing a list of public elementary schools that were engaged in open education in the State of New York. No such list existed when the study began and no such list exists today. A similar situation probably exists in most other states. We began with a list of elementary schools which were considered "open" that had been prepared for the Bureau of Elementary Curriculum Development, New York State Department of Education. The chief of this bureau, also the chairman of a task force on open education, acknowledged that the list was not exhaustive. Visits to certain schools on the list indicated that the list was not only incomplete, but that numerous schools listed were not engaged in any innovative projects.

We visited all public elementary schools that came to our attention except those in the New York City standard metropolitan area. Two schools were selected from New York City and two from Long Island. The names of the two New York City schools were obtained from Lillian Weber, director of City College Advisory Service to Open Corridors, City College of New York. She considered the two schools representative of the schools in the colleges' network. The names of the two schools visited in Long Island were obtained from the Bureau of Elementary Curriculum Development, New York State Department of Education. School officials from school districts visited in Long

49

Island indicated that they were typical of other open education schools in the immediate locale.

Since no reliable list of schools engaged in open education exists at the present time, no claim is made as to having visited a specific percentage of schools experimenting with open education in the state. On the basis of conversations with dozens of persons recognized as knowledgeable in open education, however, we believe that we visited most schools seriously engaged in open education in the state, with the exception of the New York City standard metropolitan area.

Since there is no generally accepted definition of open education, we developed criteria from the descriptions of open education advanced by persons prominent in the field.[2] The criteria were derived from the works of Blackie, Brown and Precious, Featherstone, Rathbone, Rogers, and Weber.[3] We excluded proponents of free schools (Neill, Goodman, Illich, Kozol[4]) solely because there seemed little likelihood that Americans would be willing to adopt what are considered revolutionary changes in the foreseeable future.[5]

Initially sixty-eight characteristics were derived from several prominent authors in the movement. This original list included some free school advocates such as Neill and some historical references such as Dewey. After distilling these sixty-eight characteristics to ten, the list was pilot tested at the Margaret M. Sibley School for Research and Demonstration, State University College of Arts and Science, Plattsburgh, New York. A new and final list of criteria, represented by Figure 5-1, emerged from the pilot test.

We visited each school in the sample for a period of time ranging from two hours and five minutes to six hours and forty-five minutes. We visited all classrooms considered "open" by the principal and sometimes all classrooms in the school. We talked with principals before and after visiting classrooms. Principals acted frequently as guides so the discussions were often in excess of an hour. We often conversed casually with teachers and students.

Upon leaving each school, we rated its open education program on the sixteen criteria and added any additional comments pertinent to the investigation. These narratives were often several pages in length. The criteria instrument was restricted to that segment of the school designated as "open" by the principal. If a school had twenty teachers and six hundred students engaged in open education, only the latter were rated on the criteria.

Three investigators participated in the study. To check investigator reliability, two of the investigators began by visiting two schools together, rating them independently on the criteria. Concerning investigator reliability, it should be noted that the principal investigator visited ten of the fifteen schools in the sample, eight alone and two with the second investigator. Delimitations of the study are discussed in the notes for this chapter.[6]

It may appear that a descriptive study would be less useful than a study comparing open education and traditional education classrooms. Such a study was deliberately rejected for three reasons. One, there is no definitive list of open education classrooms in the State of New York (nor in the United States), so a random sample would be impossible to obtain. Two, there is no absolute definition of open education. Currently much discussion concerns which label to attach to the concept—open education, free schools, integrated day, informal education, open corridor, the developmental classroom, etc.—rather than if it is a concept and, if so, its essential characteristics. Third, open education is a new concept that has yet to be developed fully. If a comparative study were conducted and revealed that traditional schools were more effective, the data would be rendered essentially useless with the simple statement that "on the first run the horse beat the train." Nothing would be more superfluous, if not destructive, than to conduct comparative studies concerning innovations that have not been in existence long enough to reach their potential.

Findings

We report the findings as follows: (1) scores of individual schools on criteria; (2) scores of all schools for each criterion; (3) scores on criteria by schools by type of community (urban, suburban, rural); (4) scores on criteria of schools by socioeconomic level of school population; (5) additional findings.

1. Scores of Individual Schools on Criteria

The scores of individual schools on the sixteen criteria of open education ranged from a high of 78 (mean of 4.88) to a low of 38 (mean of 2.38). The highest possible raw score was 80 (mean of 5.00); the lowest possible raw score was 16 (mean of 1.00).

2. Scores of All Schools for Each Criterion

The scores of individual criterion ranged from a high of 58 to a low of 42. The lowest possible score was 16. The lowest score on the five-point scale was 1, thus a score of 1 on the sixteen criteria would be 16. A perfect score would be 16 x 5, or 80. Scores were as follows:

Room Arrangement	58
Affective Environment	58
Instruction	58
Evaluation of Students	58
Noise Level	57

Figure 5-1. Instrument for Determining Openness of Elementary Schools

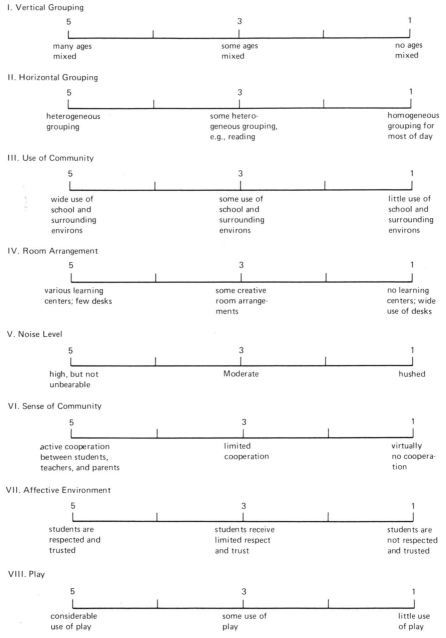

I. Vertical Grouping

5	3	1
many ages mixed	some ages mixed	no ages mixed

II. Horizontal Grouping

5	3	1
heterogeneous grouping	some hetero-geneous grouping, e.g., reading	homogeneous grouping for most of day

III. Use of Community

5	3	1
wide use of school and surrounding environs	some use of school and surrounding environs	little use of school and surrounding environs

IV. Room Arrangement

5	3	1
various learning centers; few desks	some creative room arrange-ments	no learning centers; wide use of desks

V. Noise Level

5	3	1
high, but not unbearable	Moderate	hushed

VI. Sense of Community

5	3	1
active cooperation between students, teachers, and parents	limited cooperation	virtually no coopera-tion

VII. Affective Environment

5	3	1
students are respected and trusted	students receive limited respect and trust	students are not respected and trusted

VIII. Play

5	3	1
considerable use of play	some use of play	little use of play

Figure 5-1 (cont.)

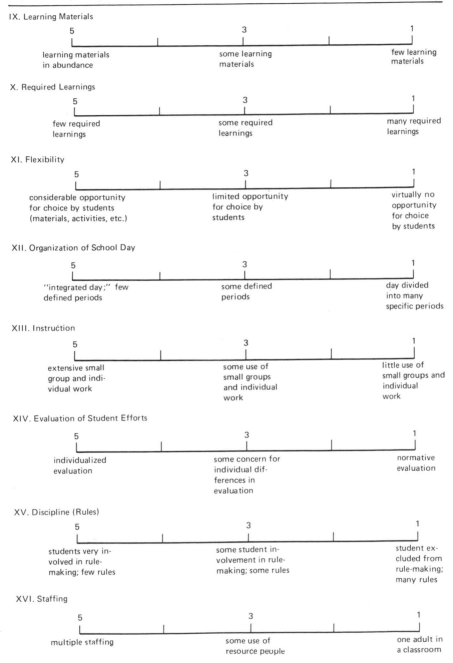

IX. Learning Materials

5	3	1
learning materials in abundance	some learning materials	few learning materials

X. Required Learnings

5	3	1
few required learnings	some required learnings	many required learnings

XI. Flexibility

5	3	1
considerable opportunity for choice by students (materials, activities, etc.)	limited opportunity for choice by students	virtually no opportunity for choice by students

XII. Organization of School Day

5	3	1
"integrated day;" few defined periods	some defined periods	day divided into many specific periods

XIII. Instruction

5	3	1
extensive small group and individual work	some use of small groups and individual work	little use of small groups and individual work

XIV. Evaluation of Student Efforts

5	3	1
individualized evaluation	some concern for individual differences in evaluation	normative evaluation

XV. Discipline (Rules)

5	3	1
students very involved in rule-making; few rules	some student involvement in rule-making; some rules	student excluded from rule-making; many rules

XVI. Staffing

5	3	1
multiple staffing	some use of resource people	one adult in a classroom

Staffing	57
Horizontal Grouping	56
Learning Materials	56
Play	55
Sense of Community	54
Student Involvement in Rules	52
Flexibility	51
Organization of School Day	51
Use of Community	48
Required Learnings	46
Vertical Grouping	42

I. Vertical Grouping. Schools scoring 4 or 5 were normally engaged in multiage grouping (placing students of different grades or ages together). Schools scoring 1 placed students in a specific grade on the basis of age. The schools scoring 4 and 5 had an average score of 58.8 on the criteria and a mean score of 53.8. The scores on this criterion were bimodal with seven schools scoring 4 or 5, and six schools scoring 1.

II. Horizontal Grouping. Some teachers avoided grouping the students by ability, but most had some groupings during the day based upon ability. Five schools scored 4 or 5 in this criterion while all others scored 3.

III. Use of Community. This criterion referred to the students' ability to leave the classroom to visit other areas of the school, and teachers' and students' use of the community as a place for learning.

Use of community scores covered the entire range. The total score of 48 (third lowest) indicates that there is not an inordinate use of the community in the open education classrooms we visited. Students tended to remain in their classrooms except in a few schools in which there was considerable use of corridors. It should be noted that open corridor schools do not necessarily provide children access to the corridors. Some have teachers assigned to the corridor, and the corridors often become "just" another classroom.

There is relatively little use of the community. When the investigators asked school personnel about the use of the outdoors, a common reply was that teachers used the outdoors extensively. But when pursued for specifics, examples principals and teachers cited were fairly stereotyped, such as field trips to the supermarket. Teachers in open classrooms probably did make more field trips and local nature walks than the average teacher, but the difference did not appear to be significant. In this regard, children in one school were permitted to walk anywhere they wished in the school if they had a ROAMER's sign around their necks. While the activity has merit, it also suggests that children might be stopped and questioned if found in the corridors without a ROAMER's sign.

IV. Room Arrangement. Twelve of the fifteen schools had flexible room arrangements. Tables were used in most schools. When tables were not used, desks were pushed together to serve as work areas. Desks were in rows in only two schools. In one school, it was reported that "rooms were creative and chaotic. Animals, rugs on floor for sitting, old overstuffed furniture. Homey was the word for this place."

Many classrooms did not have a teacher's desk. When a desk was used, it was normally piled high with instructional materials and situated in a corner of the room. Only two schools had teachers' desks at the front of the room.

V. Noise Level. This criterion was included because almost all authors concerned with open education state that children are active and consequently noisy in open classrooms. While some quiet time is necessary and desirable, children generally are noisy when working in groups.

The schools with the six highest scores in all criteria had 5 in this criterion. The schools with the six lowest scores had ratings of 4, 3, 2. The noise level was high in most schools, but in general not so high that teachers could not talk with small groups of children or children could not converse with fellow schoolmates. We cannot recall one instance where the noise level was too high for productive work, although in a couple of cases, the teachers seemed to think it was too noisy. Such responses may have been prompted by the presence of the investigators.

VI. Sense of Community. There was considerable talk of community involvement in several schools and, in four, it had become a reality. Parents hired or served as paraprofessionals and essentially hired the professional staff. This was decidedly not the case in every school. Scores varied on this criterion but tended to cluster around 3.

VII. Affective Environment. We sought data from two sources. First, the overall *geist* of the school as evidenced by the respect accorded children by all personnel in the school, student access to the corridors, the outward appearance of the corridors, the existence or absence of signs such as "Report to the Principal's Office Before Entering the School." Second, the attitude of teachers as evidenced by the amount of trust and respect shown toward children, as well as the amount of touching, hugging, and laughing.

Ten schools scored 4 or 5 on this criterion. One investigator noted that at least fifteen children said hello to the principal in a brief visit to one classroom. In another instance, three children jumped on a male teacher as he was walking down the corridor. The teacher seemed to enjoy it. Another investigator noted that "children touch and are touched, yell and are yelled at."

VIII. Play. We frequently encountered children engaged in play or activities of an unscheduled nature in which no expectations are made of the outcomes. Children might be building with blocks or chasing a hamster. Scores varied from 2 to 5 on this criterion. Seldom did one see an inactive child in schools that scored high on the criterion. There was also a considerable degree of activity in the schools that scored in the middle range. At a minimum, the children seemed happy to be in school. Most of the schools visited were enjoyable places for children to spend their time.

IX. Learning Materials. With the exception of four schools, there were considerable learning materials in evidence. Scores ranged from 1 to 5. Some classrooms were literally so full of materials that it was difficult to walk through. Many of these materials were the products of children's efforts, although commercially-made materials were available as well. One investigator commented:

The classrooms were extremely messy. There is old furniture, bleachers, old rugs, and pillows apparently donated by the parents and dragged-in by the kids. The latest addition were room dividers made of orange crates. There is old electronic equipment, games, books, bilingual workshops, etc. Classrooms were bombarded with real learning activities going on. Students are in reading corners, repairing toasters and televisions, painting and drawing, working math problems with Cuisenaire rods and other materials.

Rarely did one see a textbook or workbook, and in only two schools were the children engaged in the same activity (at the same level) at the same time. Both of these schools scored low on the criterion. Animals were in abundance, as were aquaria and terraria. Cooking utensils were found in most classrooms or a kitchen was readily available.

X. Required Learnings. While there appeared to be less emphasis on the organization of what was to be taught, it seemed as if most teachers and children knew what was required of them, and they expected to comply with some required learnings. Some teachers gave verbal testimony to the effect that, "We don't believe that every child has to learn how to read and write by age six," but these same teachers were working with children on their reading skills. The investigator who visited the school that seemed the most "open" said it this way, "Children learn reading and mathematics by the time they leave the school, but no one is quite sure how (or why). There exists an *implicit* feeling, stemming from the principal among others, that certain skills should be learned by boys and girls."

Not one school scored 5 in this criterion. This might seem somewhat surprising since there is reason to believe the sample included some of the most innovative classrooms in the state. This is discussed more thoroughly in the next section. By contrast, no school scored 1; thus all ratings were either 2, 3, or 4.

XI. Flexibility. Flexibility is concerned with the degree of choice offered children in selecting materials and activities. No clearly discernible pattern was available from the sample. Some teachers offered considerable choice while others seemed to structure activities rather closely. The scores ranged from 1 to 5.

XII. Organization of School Day. Every school visited had some activity that was scheduled for all children. In some instances, reading was at a specific time for all children. In other instances, a block of time was set aside for any activity that appeared worthwhile to the students or teachers. In general, the organization of the school day was flexible. The school day was not broken up into discrete time segments as those found in most traditional classrooms. The organization allowed for free time so children could pursue interests of their choice, although teachers did considerable guiding of children into activities they thought worthwhile. All but five schools scored 4 or 5 on this criterion.

XIII. Instruction. There was considerable individual and small group work. It was not unusual to find the teacher sitting on the floor working with an individual child. Small groups of children would work together in what seemed like independent work but was being monitored usually by a teacher. In only two schools did we observe a teacher in front of the room talking to an entire class.

This criterion differentiated clearly the high from the low scoring schools. Five of the top six scoring schools scored 5, and the remaining one scored 4. Four of the five lowest scoring schools scored 2 or 3, with the remaining one scoring 4.

XIV. Evaluation of Student Efforts. Teachers and principals questioned the wisdom of using normative standards of evaluation with children. While virtually all persons gave verbal testimony to that effect, conversations with children as well as a review of reporting practices revealed that individualized or criterion-based evaluation had not replaced normative evaluation in all schools. All but two schools retained report cards. All schools had some form of parent-teacher conference. The scores varied from 2 to 5 on this criterion.

XV. Discipline (Rules). We were concerned largely with the nature of discipline and the number of rules in this criterion. Most schools had few rules other than those involving safety. Safety rules were kept to a minimum as many teachers thought a risk-free school undesirable; thus, children baked though they could be burned, sawed though they could be cut.

When punishment was necessary, it was normally depriving the child of some desired activity. One principal indicated that he spanked children. A child in one school confided to one investigator that the principal "kicks us in the butt, in his office, when we misbehave." Many teachers indicated that discipline was far less of a problem in traditional than in open education classrooms. Eleven schools scored 3 or 4 on this criterion.

XVI. Staffing. Some open classrooms had a single teacher while others had multiple staffing consisting of several aides, paid or volunteer. Of the six schools with the highest total scores, five scored 5 and one scored 4 on this criterion. Significantly, however, two schools with the lowest total scores also scored 4 and 5. It is not certain then whether multiple staffing is an essential component of open education. We encountered many teacher aides, but aides are fairly evident throughout the state.

3. Scores on Criteria by Schools by
Type of Community (Urban, Suburban, Rural)

The scores on criteria by school were analyzed by type of community. The mean score on open education criteria for schools in urban communities was 62; in suburban communities, 57; in semirural or rural communities, 49. No school in a semirural or rural community scored as high as those in urban communities.

4. Scores on Criteria of Schools by
Socioeconomic Level of School Population

Scores on criteria of schools were analyzed by socioeconomic level of population. Socioeconomic level was divided into three distinct categories—above middle class, middle class, and below middle class. We normally determined socioeconomic level of the community by asking as many persons as possible, as well as observing the nature of the community. In most instances, we relied on the judgment of the principal.

Above middle class communities had a mean score of 59; middle class communities had a mean score of 50; below middle class communities had a mean score of 60. The range in above middle class communities is from 78 (two points from a perfect score) to 38. The range of middle class and lower middle class is not nearly so large.

5. Additional Findings

(1) The lack of agreement on a definition of open education in the State of New York stems in part from the reluctance of authors prominent in the movement to define the concept clearly. This concept, if indeed it is a discrete notion at all,

is known by several terms from "open corridors" to "integrated day." The confusion concerning the terms can be found in the various bureaus concerned with open education in the State Department of Education. This lack of specificity not only permeates the State Department of Education, but universities and colleges in the state as well.

There is evidence that some schools are labeling themselves open or informal without changing significantly their educational program. Some schools believe open education is synonymous with free schools, open space design, multiage grouping, individualized instruction, or a variety of other concepts and slogans.

(2) We found no significant difference among the scores of schools varying in size of total student enrollment. On the criteria, the mean score of schools with enrollments between 83 and 160 was 65.2; with enrollments between 400 and 689, 53.1; and with enrollments between 800 and 1,100, 60.2 While there was a slight difference between the scores of small and large schools, the difference is not significant enough to confirm the contention of some persons that elementary schools should have small enrollments. The two schools scoring 78 on the criteria had student enrollments of 160 and 900. The two schools scoring 66 and 65 points respectively had student enrollments of 633 and 550.

(3) Principals and teachers from virtually every school voiced concern about the objections of some citizens and parents to open education. In one urban community, citizens had confused open education with busing, and the board of education was considering closing the school during the coming academic year to placate the parents. We considered this school as one of the better schools in the sample.

The concern of citizens was usually centered on whether the children were learning the three Rs, and that children were given too much independent time.

(4) Open education was schoolwide in only four of the fifteen schools in the sample.

(5) All schools gave parents the option to enroll their children in either open or traditional classrooms.

(6) Open education is being practiced primarily in the early elementary grades.

(7) Only three of the fifteen schools were engaged in a systematic evaluation of their program. In the remaining twelve schools, there were no systematic evaluations, although many teachers had reservations and doubts about some aspects of their programs.

(8) No attempt was made to determine the competence of teachers in open education classrooms. We did not seek the principals' views concerning the competence of teachers nor determine the teachers' years of experience working with children. On the basis of conversations with teachers and observations in classrooms, we believe that the open education classroom teachers were far more competent than the average teacher in the State of New York.

(9) Historically, there has been much discussion in the State of New York

between the quality of education upstate and downstate. Downstate is the heavily populated standard metropolitan area of New York City, extending northward to include the hundreds of suburbs that may be thirty miles away. Upstate includes the remainder of the state which is entirely rural except for a half dozen urban centers.

Upstate and downstate schools did not differ significantly so far as their scores on the open education criteria were concerned. The seven downstate schools scored 58.4 on the open education criteria; the eight upstate schools scored 56.1. If one excludes the semirural and rural communities from the upstate data, upstate scores representing urban and suburban communities would be increased to 63.

(10) While the support and adoption of open education apparently continue to increase, the actual percentage of teachers engaged in open education remains very small—perhaps less than five percent. It is possible that we overlooked schools engaged in open education (there may be fifty in the New York City area alone), but the five percent figure still seems probable.

(11) While we frequently found classrooms in which children worked placidly and the teacher was relaxed, more often we observed a teacher extremely busy, trying to work with one student while several others gathered around for assistance. In some cases, we could not understand how one human being could tolerate such an environment for approximately one thousand hours a year. This is not meant to suggest that the classrooms were chaotic nor that the teaching was ineffective, only that the degree of activity was often so intense that many teachers must have been exhausted by the end of the day. Several teachers indicated that they were extremely tired, and one consultant appeared to be overworked and on the verge of exhaustion.

Analysis

We found that, on the average, children were active, happy, and interested in the activities in which they were engaged. The classrooms, on the average, were messy, filled with instructional materials, many student-made projects, and lacking in textbooks and workbooks. The teachers, on the average, were active—working with individual students or small groups of students. They appeared interested in students, personable, and dedicated.

We did not visit traditional schools, so we cannot make comparisons from empirical data to open education classrooms. If one accepts, however, the educational program espoused by Dewey, the legions of researchers and practitioners who advocate "learning by doing," individualized or small group instruction, more freedom of choice for children, process learning, the use of many instructional materials by children, earnest and loving teachers, and student-made projects, then one is inclined to believe that children were indeed learning more in the open classrooms visited.

While traditional classrooms were not visited, we are familiar with research studies conducted during the past few years concerning the status of traditional schools. Silberman's comprehensive study of elementary and secondary schools, to mention the most prominent, paints a bleak picture indeed.[7]

Goodlad, Klein, and associates visited 158 classrooms in 67 schools. Their observations pertain to 150 of these classrooms—32 kindergarten, 45 first grade, 26 second grade, 18 third grade, and 29 classes at three grade levels classified as "special." They found that classrooms and schools are much the same as they had been twenty years ago, and in some instances not as good as they were forty years ago.[8] The findings of Goodlad and Klein are particularly distressing since the classrooms visited were kindergarten through grade three, generally considered to be more child oriented and less repressive than higher grades.

The criteria that had high scores were room arrangement, affective environment, instruction, evaluation of students, noise level, staffing, learning materials, play, and sense of community. We would conclude, therefore, that these are essential characteristics of open education. The three lowest scores, however, are worth examining.

The lowest score on the criteria was 42, vertical grouping. One is inclined to conclude that this is the least relevant of the criteria of open education. In this study, vertical grouping was not equated with nongradedness or individualized instruction, but solely with whether children from different grades or of different ages were deliberately placed in multiage groupings.

While multiage grouping has been espoused by several educator-evangelists (educators normally of national prominence who advance innovations because they *appear* to be desirable for children), research studies have yet to be conducted to demonstrate the usefulness of such a practice. In this regard, any graded classroom has children of different ages and different achievement levels, so every classroom is already multiage grouped. On the basis of data from this study, we believe multiage grouping, while perhaps desirable, is not a critical factor in any type of educational program.

The second lowest score on the criteria of open education was 43, required learnings. While some principals and teachers talked about overemphasizing basic skills, none was prepared to say that some learnings should not be required. Instead of not requiring basic skills, the emphasis seemed to be on toning them down, freeing the student to proceed at his own pace, and being more alert to the readiness of the child. But if a child did not respond appropriately in what appeared to be a reasonable time, a teacher intervened. In this respect, open education is far different from Neill's Summerhill, but not significantly different from many so-called free schools in the United States.[9]

The third lowest score was use of community—freeing the environment of the classroom to permit the child to use the entire school facility and the facilities outside the school. As reported in the findings this was not much in evidence and seldom mentioned by teachers. While use of community seems logical, data from this study indicate that it is not an essential component of an open education program.

Were the schools we visited "really" engaged in open education? Certainly many persons suspect that some so-called open education schools are not open and have merely attached the label to the school. A few schools we visited scrupulously avoided the label, though in fact they scored high on our criteria of open education. Since open education is multidimensional, that is, it includes a variety of characteristics such as curriculum, instruction, and student evaluation, it is difficult to measure. It cannot be assumed that open education means the same thing to all persons involved.

The list of criteria is an attempt to be more precise in considering open education. The use of criteria, however, does not determine if a school is truly open. One would be inclined to agree, for example, that schools one and two, which scored 78 of a possible 80 points are quite open, at least to the degree that the criteria are valid. But can the same be said for schools three and four, whose scores were 66 and 65 respectively? Perhaps, but what about schools eight, nine, and ten whose scores were 55, 53, and 52 respectively? It could be argued, for example, that school fifteen was open even though it scored 38.

We are inclined to believe that schools numbered ten through fifteen are not open in any substantial sense. This would place the cutoff point on the criteria at 51. Regardless of the obvious hazards of a single figure, so long as persons do not view it as arbitrary or magical, it could serve some useful purpose.

Open education is being implemented more at the elementary grades than in higher grades. There are several possible explanations for this. Citizens and parents are more amenable to letting children have a "good time" in their early years. They are not as concerned when their child returns home and says he played with clay all day or had a birthday party. This is in part because many parents consider early elementary education comparatively unimportant (kindergarten is considered a play time to many parents). It may also be that parents themselves are beginning to resist the urge to accelerate growth that is occasioned by a highly technological society. They may wish to preserve their children's youth for a few more years. While children can learn concepts at an early age, there is the growing feeling, stimulated in part by the work of Piaget, that many concepts should be postponed until later when they can be learned in a shorter period of time. In addition, as Myers points out in Chapter 7, the integration of disciplines into a variety of projects is far easier in the elementary than secondary schools.

While there is a tendency for open education to decrease as the age of the child and the grade level increase, this is not necessarily the most logical process. In fact, a strong argument can be made that young children require less "openness" and more structure than older children. Andreae believes, for example, that open education classrooms are more structured than traditional classrooms. While such a notion is not intended to justify rigidly-constructed first-grade classrooms, it does suggest that schooling might better become more free, not less, as the student matures. New York City's "mini" high schools and the Empire State College in New York State are examples of increased student freedom at higher levels of schooling.

Few schools engaged in open education have a systematic evaluation of their program. This is unfortunate. Rigorous comparative research studies of emerging innovations should be avoided. Boards of education should assiduously avoid demanding that children in open education classrooms achieve equal to or better than children in traditional classrooms. Nonetheless, school personnel, particularly those who occupy positions at the central office level and above, should arrange for descriptive studies aimed at evaluating the program. Such data could include the number of books checked out of the library, student and teacher absenteeism, number and nature of discipline problems, creativeness of student projects, and maintenance costs. Standardized achievement tests could be used as well, provided they measure what the teachers are seeking to achieve. If the scores of standardized achievement tests were significantly less in open education classrooms, there would be cause for concern; but, if there were no significant difference, there would be merit to retaining open education.

Evaluation should not be seen as an invisible Sword of Damocles, ever poised to strike down the unfortunate innovation that fails to meet expectations. New programs need time to develop. Open education in England has been evolving for over forty years. For modifications and improvements to occur, however, some basis for ongoing data collection should be made.

We believe that open education will enjoy widespread and uncritical verbal acceptance by most educators in the State of New York. It will dominate discussions in the field of education at least during the first half of the seventies, if not longer, although it will probably have a shorter history than progressive education. It will be written about by advocates and inevitably by critics. It will attract the attention of educational researchers.

On the basis of our visits to 122 open education classrooms from Coney Island to Buffalo, we do not foresee any significant and permanent positive gain for teachers and children as a result of open education in the State of New York. This is not because open education is undesirable. Some open education classrooms have developed an extremely impressive educational program. The reason open education will not be a vital force for the improvement of education is because few models worthy of emulation exist. When such models evolve (some already have), there is every reason to believe they will be rejected by many teachers. There is abundant data available already to suggest that many who espouse it will misinterpret it and be subject to peer and parent disapproval. The human resources to make open education a widespread and permanent educational system are lacking, and there appears little evidence to suggest the situation will change significantly in the immediate future, if at all.

Alternative Schools

Daniel Linden Duke

For years it has been popular to deride public schools for offering only custodial care or babysitting services to American families. Beginning in the mid-sixties parents, teachers, and students began to replace words with action. At first, efforts were directed toward reform within existing public schools. Changes such as team teaching, individualized instruction, and more relevant courses were introduced. The most comprehensive of these reforms has been open education which embodies extensive modfications in the organization of time, space, learning materials, students, and staff. Open education, however, is still a reform. It does not constitute a major alteration in the way schools are structured or a fundamental critique of American society.

Alternative Schools

Alternative elementary and secondary schools constitute not only a condemnation of what and how public schools teach, as do open schools, but also a challenge to how they are organized and governed. The rapid development of free schools, street academies, schools within schools, schools without walls, and minischools represents sweeping changes.

Historically, schools deemed "alternative" or innovative did not offer new organizational forms, but rather a unique curriculum or radical instructional technique. Parochial schools added religious training. Elitist private schools provided didactic classroom instruction with heavy emphasis on knowledge essential for the development of "character." A handful of public and nonpublic schools attempted to implement the enlightened pedagogical ideas of such persons as Montessori, Froebel, Dewey, and Piaget.

Now, for the first time, students of average or below average socioeconomic status are being granted real options in their schooling. Parents have become involved along with teachers in establishing new schools. Public school systems that previously had been willing or able to provide alternatives only within a given school, and usually for a specific type of student, are beginning to establish alternative schools open to all. Recent schools encompass progressive and even radical beliefs, whereas traditional alternative or "private" schools largely reflected sectarian and conservative values.

65

Schools distinguished as "alternative" share two common traits: (1) the school is accessible by choice rather than by assignment, and (2) they profess to embody substantive differences in curriculum, instructional methods, and/or school organization.

Widespread dissatisfaction on the part of parents, students, and teachers is responsible for the appearance of between 300 and 400 new schools with these characteristics since the mid-sixties.[1] Dissatisfaction with conventional schools has existed for decades, based upon the public school's perceived failure to acknowledge individual differences, provide relevant and humane instruction, and encourage initiative and cooperation among students. Rarely, though, was discontent concerned with the basic structure of the school—its decision-making processes, roles, and methods of organization.

People are still dissatisfied with public schools. Some have begun to understand the problems encountered by earlier reformers. The progressive education movement of the twenties and thirties embodied many of the pedagogical notions espoused by current advocates of alternative schools. Many persons are discovering that good teaching is good teaching, whether it occurs in P.S. 150, a suburban open classroom, or a rural free school.[2] Reflective critics of contemporary public education are realizing that many changes demanded now by parents and students have been implemented already in many public school systems. The actual appearance of *public* alternative schools is testimony to the lengths some public school systems will go to mollify the discontent conveyed in parent activism and in such impressive critiques as Silberman's *Crisis in the Classroom.*

Pedagogical Dimensions

It is important to note that the changes embodied in many public alternative schools are limited to matters of curriculum, instruction, evaluation, and student organization—the pedagogical dimensions of schooling. Some public alternative schools, including those in New York City, Philadelphia, Ithaca, Arlington, and Berkeley, have attempted nonpedagogical or structural changes as well. Why these particular cities have fostered such extensive changes is not understood fully, but reasons may include the availability of federal or local funds and the political makeup of the community.[3]

It is surprising to the person visiting alternative schools that they are so similar.[4] Naturally, a minischool in New York City differs from a free school in the California foothills. Nonetheless, that minischool resembles a street academy in Chicago, while the West Coast free school is not unlike an independent school in Cambridge, Massachusetts. There is no intention to plant the label of "conformity" on alternative schools. However, it is necessary to realize that Afro-American history, yoga, and organic gardening are not unique to any one alternative school. Small, private, elementary alternatives enjoy no monopoly on flexible scheduling of so-called undifferentiated days. Utilizing the city as a classroom—exploring hospitals, museums, and factories—is not an exclusive feature of large public programs. On the basis of a review of the literature and extensive visitation, the following pedagogical characteristics seem to fit a large number of recent alternative schools, both public and nonpublic:

1. A wide range of individual options including what, when, where, and how to learn.
2. Increased emphasis on affective development.
3. Multiple-staffing involving teacher aides, assistants, volunteers, parents, resource people, etc.
4. Some attempt to group students of different ages, abilities, and/or home backgrounds.
5. Nontraditional facilities ranging from old homes to schools without walls.
6. Wide use of learning environments outside the school.
7. More individually-based, as opposed to normative, evaluation.
8. A general climate of warmth, informality, and cooperation.

Since nonpublic alternative schools appeared several years before most public alternative schools, it would seem that the former, despite their numerical insignificance, have exerted a considerable influence on public education. In one area, though, nonpublic alternative schools have prompted little change in their public counterparts. The failure of many public alternative schools to implement basic structural alterations may suggest a difference in perceptions between those outside the system and those within. Significant pedagogical innovations from discovery learning to open education constitute reforms rather than revolutions. They represent radical means to traditional objectives. The failure of public alternative schools to undergo basic changes in decision-making structure and role definition should not be obscured by public relations terminology like the child-centered school, humanistic education, parent involvement, and freedom of choice. Slogans and idealistic proclamations conceal the fact that new ways of organizing children and adults, new operational values, new notions of professionalism, new processes of decision making, and new structural relationships between school and community have not been approached by public alternative schools with the same fervor as pedagogical change. Understanding the reasons for this discrepancy is one focus of this chapter. In addition, it is vital to determine what forces have prompted parents, students, and teachers—groups that have been dissatisfied for years—to begin in the sixties to establish alternative schools.

Organizational Dimensions and Roles

Alternative schools are organizations of people. They embody goals which are articulated in varying degrees of specificity. The achievement of these goals and the coordination of the people involved in their achievement require decisions to be made at a number of levels. In an earlier study, I contend that decision making is the critical element of any organization.[5] I posit six types of decisions that are made in a school:

1. *Long-range planning and policy decisions*, including decisions concerning school philosophy, goals, types of student, building facility, administration, personnel, and major programmatic changes.
2. *Daily operational decisions*, including decisions about projects, individual assignments, field trips, interpersonal problems, counseling, minor modifications of the environment, scheduling, and general classroom management.
3. *Budgetary decisions*, including decisions concerning appropriations, distribution, and funding.
4. *Disciplinary decisions*, including decisions about school rules and the treatment of those found disobeying them.
5. *Curricular decisions*, including decisions on course offerings, topics for group examination, organization of intended learnings, required learnings, and appropriateness of subject matter.
6. *Instructional decisions*, including decisions concerning who will teach what, which methods will be used, how students will be organized, how resources will be arranged, and how learning will be evaluated.

The distinction between these types of decisions is not always clear. Frequently curricular decisions and daily operational decisions cannot be distinguished. A further caution concerns the fact that the existence of six "ideal type" decisions does not mean that all people involved in schools recognize their existence, not to mention their discreteness. The decision-making model is intended only to facilitate discussion of the organization of alternative schools.

Decisions involve one or a combination of persons. Where a specific or formal decision-making process exists, those involved normally are indicated in terms of role—student, teacher, trustee, principal, etc. While generalizations about schools are hazardous, there is some value to presenting a tentative model of decision making in a typical public school. The following persons or groups tend to be involved:

Long-range decisions: Board of education, superintendent and central administration, consultants, principals, teacher unions.
Budgetary decisions: Board of education, taxpayers, superintendent, principals, teacher unions.
Curricular decisions: Superintendent and central administration, department heads, teachers.
Daily operational decisions: Principals, department heads, teachers.
Disciplinary decisions: Board of education, principals and vice . principals, teachers.
Instructional decisions: Supervisors of instruction, principals, teachers.

Students are absent entirely from the formal or publicly acknowledged decision-making structure. Parents as a group are involved only in voting for boards, bonds, and budgets. They exercise basically negative powers, i.e., they can reject but rarely initiate. While teachers appear in four out of six categories, their influence is proportionate to the strength of their union and their personal rapport with administrators. Wayland concludes that the teacher

is a functionary in an essentially bureaucratic system. As such, he is a replaceable unit in a rationally organized system, and most of the significant aspects of work are determined for him. Any areas in which he makes decisions are those which are given to him and are not inherent in his role as teacher. They may therefore be altered, increased, or removed completely.[6]

Similarly, Anderson notes that teachers distribute little decision-making power to students because the teachers themselves receive so little from school administrators.[7] Decision making in public education is fundamentally a bureaucratic process, complete with centralization of authority and specialization of function.

New Styles of Decision Making in Public Alternative Schools. Alternative public schools represent several departures from conventional school decision making. (1) Many public alternative schools are funded by federal monies (ESEA titled funds and grants from the Experimental Schools Program), state funds, and private foundation grants. Many decisions thus can be influenced by outside agencies. (2) Due in part to the fact that public alternative schools often attract dynamic, independent teachers from within public education, they tend to be staffed by professionals willing and able to assume greater autonomy from the central administration. To some extent this new authority is shared with students. In addition, gains in responsibility have their price. Teachers sometimes take a cut in salary and an augmented work load. (3) Public alternative schools embody fewer official rules. The result is less debatable topics and, consequently, a decrease in the necessity to make as many decisions.[8]

New Styles of Decision Making in Nonpublic Alternative Schools. Despite the significant changes in decision making in public alternatives, they still fall short of the organizational innovations encompassed by many nonpublic alternative schools. (1) There are fewer formal rules in nonpublic alternatives than in their public counterparts. In some cases, no official rules exist. The result is a reduction in the number of instances in which school-wide decisions must be made. The decisions needed tend to be arrived at through interaction between individual students and teachers. (2) Parents are more involved in nonpublic alternative schools, especially elementary schools. While many public alternative schools consult parents in the early stages of development and set up advisory bodies, they do not provide for significant parental participation in planning, developing, staffing, and support. Nonpublic alternative schools tend to include parents in the school community. (3) The teacher in a nonpublic alternative school is, ironically, more powerful and more vulnerable than his colleague in a public alternative school. There are far fewer administrators. In fact, there may be none at all. Being free of bureaucrats and administrative guidelines, however, means that teachers also are denied the "official channels" that serve to divert parent discontent. The nonpublic alternative school is small and intimate. Some would describe it as an educational Peyton Place. Teachers must deal with students and parents usually without the convenience of an administrator-scape-goat and a complex bureaucracy.

The effect of diminishing or eliminating a school administration and of increasing the involvement of parents, students, and teachers has been to create new roles for these individuals in nonpublic alternative schools. Where administrative roles are retained, they encompass more coordination and maintenance and less leadership and direction. In addition to these duties, head persons typically spend time teaching. In fact, teachers themselves may be administrators. It also is not uncommon to find parent volunteers, on a rotating basis, serving as administrators. Public alternative schools usually have full time directors or principals. These individuals are responsible to the local district administration and, thus, tend to be more supervisory and directive.

Teachers

The role of teachers in alternative schools often undergoes drastic redefinition. Caught between the demands of bureaucratization and the dictates of professionalism, the public school teacher finds little freedom from role confusion in alternative schools.[9] In public education, professionalism dictates particularism—the necessity for dealing with students on an individual basis. Simultaneously, the school bureaucracy, as embodied in the central administration and the principal, encourages universalism—the capacity to relate to all students in the same, impersonal way. In public and nonpublic alternative schools, teachers generally are *expected* to relate to students in a highly individualized manner.

Instead of specialized academic competence, a hallmark of professionalism, teachers also are expected to be generalists, especially in nonpublic alternative schools. Instead of loyalty to the school as an organization, an expectation of public school employees, teachers in nonpublic alternative schools are encouraged to feel a primary commitment to the local community and the students.

The teacher is far less secure in a nonpublic alternative school. Financially, these schools exist with few reserves. The withdrawal of several students may jeopardize the stability of the entire organization. On another level, teacher insecurity can result from being subjected to personal interactions with parents and students. Public schools often discourage these relationships. Having to deal frequently and honestly with parents and students opens the alternative school teacher to criticism. Because of the nature of many parents who become involved in new schools, the teacher may be criticized by someone with greater expertise than himself. In addition, many teachers who prepared for their careers in schools of education discover that these credentials are viewed more as a liability than as an asset in many instances. What once served as the basis for teacher status is accorded little value in a nonpublic alternative school.

Despite these problems, the number of teachers desiring to "drop out" of conventional public schools is burgeoning. Nonpublic alternative schools promise potentially great rewards in terms of personal satisfaction and freedom from administrative supervision. Public alternative schools offer equal satisfaction, though less freedom and not so great a feeling of participation in a "radical" experiment.

Parents

Nonpublic alternative schools promise parents a wide variety of roles that are inaccessible in public schools. They may serve as teachers, students, volunteers, assistants, bus drivers, resource people, clerks, scroungers for material, administrators, janitors, fund raisers, and representatives of school government. Parent involvement tends to be greater in elementary schools. In many cases, the newly acquired responsibilities prove more demanding in terms of time, energy, expertise, and cost than parents had anticipated. The result is sometimes the formation of an inner circle of parents with adequate time and motivation to assume the lion's share of the burden. As these parents come to perform more tasks, they incur resentment from many parents who are unable or unwilling to participate. Perhaps because of the difficulties surrounding the coordination of parent involvement, some nonpublic alternative schools are rejecting parent participation as an organizational feature.

Adult-Student Interrelations

The relationships between adults and students are not immune from change in nonpublic alternative schools. Parents often become visible to their children during the day. Children see adults in new roles and settings. Similarly, parents gain a new perspective of their children as they watch them interact with other adults and share decision-making responsibilities.

Relations between individual students change also, though perhaps not so extensively as other relations. The small size of most alternative schools reduces a student's reservoir of friends. Frequent mixing of ages, however, brings students into closer contact with older and younger children. Cliques still develop, and sex consciousness continues to govern much of the quality of boy-girl interactions. While alternative schools actively seek a heterogeneous student body, most nonpublic alternative schools are able to attract a wide range of students. Students in alternative schools as a rule, though, enjoy less extensive, though possibly more intensive, relations with representatives of other socioeconomic classes and races.

Students

The role of the student in a nonpublic alternative school tends to undergo more extensive redefinition than in a public alternative school, largely because of the nature of the organizational structure in each. In nonpublic alternative schools students cease being primarily learners. They may be tutors or teachers. Friendships with nonrelated adults develop. At times the student is required to be a curriculum designer or an evaluator. He may participate in disciplinary decisions, rule making, and school administration. Learning to cope with more responsibility affects students in various ways. Those with many years of experience in conventional schools can find the assumption of responsibility too much of a challenge. Others welcome the opportunity to exercise initiative and influence. It seems clear that alternative schools are not designed for everybody.

Role Conflict

Whenever roles undergo extensive redefinition, the likelihood of role conflict is heightened. Getzels states that this phenomenon occurs

whenever a role incumbent is required to conform simultaneously to a number of expectations which are mutually exclusive, contradictory, or inconsistent, so that adjustment to one set of requirements makes adjustment to the other impossible or at least difficult.[10]

Teachers in nonpublic alternative schools are subject to role confusion, particularly if they have had experience in public schools. Parents and students do not escape this phenomenon either. Those alternative schools that survive the first year or two manage to minimize role conflict. Teachers accept membership as equals in the school community or they become recognized clearly as professional employees. Parents wrestle with their own participation until they can work out a relatively even distribution of responsibilities or until they can agree to leave most of the chores to the hired staff. Students who feel uncomfortable assuming considerable responsibility for their education return to public schools or traditional private institutions. Overall, the reduction of role conflict in alternative schools probably involves as much unlearning of previous roles as the learning of new ones.

If there is one aspect of new roles that clearly distinguishes them from the old, it is the very real stake that parents, teachers, and students share in the survival of the alternative school. In conventional and to a certain extent alternative public schools, the individual feels little responsibility for the continuation and success of the endeavor. Public schools will survive. In nonpublic alternative schools, each member of the school community becomes an integral part of the school's growth and success. One disruptive student or a single parent on an ego trip can make a mockery of participatory democracy or devastate a new school. The need for group solidarity and cooperation in the early period of growth is critical, since there are plenty of external problems such as building codes, fire regulations, finances, and local education regulations to sap energies and demoralize. Obviously, for a student, parent, or teacher to be so directly involved in the very existence of the school marks a radical departure from the role expectations of these individuals in public schools.

Parental Influence

Nonpublic alternative schools not only present new organizational roles, but also challenge traditional patterns of influence. From the concepts of formal and informal organization are derived *formal decision making*—publicly recognized processes by which legitimate decision makers arrive at decisions, and *informal decision making*—unofficial processes whereby decisions are influenced by particular people.[11] Pressure groups and private understandings epitomize the latter, while the former include board of education proceedings, mandates from the principal, and a teacher's determination of a student's grade.

Both conventional and alternative schools are formal organizations. As such, they embody formal and informal decision-making processes. Earlier research into the organization of alternative schools suggested that the fewer members of the organization included in formal decision making, the more informal decision making will occur.[12] Clearly there is a drive on the part of parents, teachers, and students to exert some degree of influence over decisions that affect their lives, even if such influence must be conveyed through subtle pressures, in-groups, and the playing of favorites.

By including more school members in formal decision making, nonpublic alternative schools, and to a lesser extent public alternative schools, tend to encompass less informal "influence peddling" and "background politicking." Major issues are raised in meetings of the entire school, rather than in closed meetings among a few persons. The elimination of many arbitrary or restrictive rules diminishes the number of issues about which group decisions must be made. What decisions are made arrogate to the realm of teacher-student interaction and provisions made to protect this process?

Organizational Structure

Alternative schools, particularly nonpublic alternative schools, constitute a dramatic change in the way schools are organized. This is obvious to anyone having spent a few moments in such a school. There is a noticeable lack of official channels, officious functionaries, and titles on doors. In effect, there is no bureaucracy. Riordan observes that alternative schools are concerned with procedural matters,

who makes decisions, how people relate to each other, and how the school defines itself relative to the system. . . . This emphasis is consistent with the general emphasis in alternative schools, which frequently develop out of a concern with the so-called hidden curriculum: the effect of the structure and process of schooling independent of curriculum content. Therefore, their concern is not so much with designing effective learning packages, but with creating a setting where students can play an active, creative role in deciding the direction their education should take. They wish to create a school community which is itself a model for that process in its relations with other institutions.[13]

Why should the structure of schools be of concern to educational reformers? After all, the functions of schools are supposed to be the concern of parents, students, and teachers. And the functions of an organization are expected to determine its structure.

Organizational structure has received much attention in the United States. Foster observes that a major reason for American economic success lies in its organizational ingenuity.[14] The presence of an open frontier served to siphon off labor reserves from the industrializing East. Immigration was encouraged as one antidote to the resulting labor shortage. A second effort to solve this problem encompassed new ways to organize existing workers. For decades the edge enjoyed by American business interests over foreign competition consisted, in part, of these revolutionary forms of labor organization, not to mention new ways of organizing capital. Technological advances alone do not explain American economic preeminence.

Katz registers little surprise that the American public school adopted a bureaucratic model for organization. He states that bureaucracy "provides a segmented educational structure that legitimizes and perpetuates the separation of children along class lines and ensures easier access to higher-status jobs for children of the affluent."[15]

Why was a structure adopted that served to perpetuate class distinctions? Katz suggests that timing had a lot to do with it. The public school appeared when the United States was experiencing its industrial revolution, a time when the virtues of efficiency and economy were paramount and the need for trained labor was skyrocketing. On the one hand, the public school acted as the principal producer and socializer of workers. Business leaders, on the other hand, continued for years to emanate from private schools.

By rejecting the bureaucratic structure of public schools and the paternalistic structure of traditional private schools, as well as many pedagogical features of both, nonpublic alternative schools simply are acknowledging what American businessmen have long known—the structure of an organization has a primary influence on its function. That public schools are popularly alleged to take up to fifty years to implement reputable innovations is testimony to the impact of bureaucracy on the nature of schools.[16] Originally intended to facilitate the achievement of organizational goals, the bureaucracy comes to determine those goals. The managerial machinery is singularly unresponsive to requests for change.

That the structure of school organization determines, to some significant extent, the school's function is a view relatively new to the study of education, though not to fields such as sociology and public administration. Educators accept the fact that a primary function of public schools is the preparation of students for life in a representative democracy. Yet, many of these experts fail to detect a discrepancy between this function and the clearly nondemocratic structure of the public schools. Could it be that the schools in part are responsible for the growing distance between citizens and their government? Zijderveld sees a direct relationship between bureaucratic structures and dissatisfaction in the United States:

The structures of modern society . . . have grown increasingly pluralistic and independent of man. Through an ever enlarging process of differentiation, modern society acquired a rather autonomous and abstract nature confronting the individual with strong but strange forms of control. It demands the attitudes of obedient functionaries from its inhabitants who experience its control as an unfamiliar kind of authority. That means societal control is no longer characterized by a familylike authority but dominated by bureaucratic neutrality and unresponsiveness. The individual often seems to be doomed to endure this situation passively, since the structures of society vanish in abstract air if he tries to grasp their very forces of control. No wonder that many seek refuge in one or another form of retreat.[17]

Perhaps the alternative school is such a retreat.

That bureaucracies are responsible for popular feelings of estrangement and powerlessness does not imply the existence of a masterful conspiracy to assume control of the United States. One of the ironies of bureaucracy is that individual bureaucrats do not seem to be conscious of their collective impact. Nor are they cognizant of a phenomenon known as goal displacement, wherein the perpetuation of the bureaucracy supplants the organization's original purpose.[18] In this process, matters of organizational self-interest displace the concerns of students, teachers, and parents. A new curriculum or teaching device is judged in terms of fiscal feasibility and congruence with the school's operational values, rather than in terms of its potential benefits to children or the community-at-large.

If an innovation passes the criteria of feasibility and congruence, it is then "sold" to local taxpayers on the grounds it is more effective or cheaper in the long run. Hence, secondary values like efficiency often supersede more fundamental values like freedom of choice, relevancy, or humane treatment of education. Accountability too often is interpreted in terms of dollars rather than responsiveness to student needs and interests.

The clearest evidence of goal displacement is found in compensatory alternative schools, schools catering to students who typically cannot succeed in regular public schools. The need for special educational programs to handle disabled, disadvantaged, and disturbed students has existed for years. Only when federal and state monies were made available for compensatory education did local school districts make a concerted effort to provide alternatives for these students. When the funds are exhausted, so too are the alternatives.

One Alternative or Many?

The unresponsiveness, goal displacement, and slowness to change associated with public school bureaucracy have contributed to the emergence of alternative schools that embody structural reforms as well as pedagogical innovations. Public and nonpublic alternatives differ, though, in the extent to which they renounce the tenets and forms of bureaucratic organization.[19] Public alternatives still exist within the overall structure of the local school district. As such, they cannot be said to have escaped bureaucracy entirely. Nonpublic alternative schools, however, embody radically different decision-making processes and roles. By no means is there one consistent pattern even among nonpublic alternative schools. Some writers caution against speaking of alternative schools as a single movement.[20]

Despite organizational differences among alternative schools, the fact remains that history has recorded an impressive flowering of radically different schools since the mid-sixties. Coincidence alone seems an inadequate explanation.

Throughout the United States, people have begun to talk about alternatives to not only public schools, but alternatives to marriage, organized religion, and Western rationality. Experiments with new lifestyles and forms of creative expression abound. No one alternative seems to prevail in any of these areas. This is an age of trial and error where it has become apparent that there is no one road to truth.

In an article entitled "End of the Impossible Dream," Schrag observed that the termination of the Kennedy-Johnson era signified the demise of the popular belief that complex social problems could be solved with agencies and infusions of money.[21] Social problems defy generalization. In education too the day of the simple panacea has passed. Alternative schools experiment with various structures and programs. Teachers are frustrated when asked which method they use or how they organize the curriculum. There are no simple descriptions of what occurs in an alternative school. Terms like individualized instruction or learning activity package are avoided. If the emergence of hundreds of alternative schools constitutes a movement, it is a movement away from rationalized, efficient, predictable education, rather than a movement towards a specific goal or methodology.

Within the alternative schools movement, much diversity exists. Graubard distinguishes four varieties, based on several criteria including "social class constituency and the way the political and the pedagogical aspects of the 'freedom' idea interact."[22] (1) The classical free school is epitomized by Summerhill—bucolic, familial, and apolitical.[23] Some are commune-based; others are boarding schools. All tend to be populated by middle and upper-middle class students. (2) The parent-teacher cooperative elementary school is a middle class school with a predilection for participatory democracy.[24] (3) The free high school includes a smorgasbord of new schools, including Summerhillian secondary schools, white working class high schools for dropouts and pushouts, and street academies for minority students.[25] (4) The community elementary school is a relatively large school supported by parents of lower socioeconomic status.[26]

While this typology provides a helpful introduction to alternative schooling, it is not very sophisticated. Two of the types are based on aspects of school governance; two seem to employ class as a determinant. Grade level is significant for three. The free high school actually encompasses three distinct types, all joined by a common focus on adolescent students.

An alternative to Graubard's typology is one based on the function of the school and its legal status.[27] The classical free school is retained as a distinct example. It is always nonpublic. The other alternative schools may be public or nonpublic, but they are all day schools and located in urban or suburban settings. These alternative schools are either compensatory or noncompensatory. A compensatory alternative is designed for students who cannot or are not expected to succeed in regular public schools. These students suffer a plethora of labels such as disadvantaged, culturally deprived, undermotivated, slow learner, potential dropout, emotionally disturbed, or remedial. There have been compensatory alternatives since the pauper schools of the nineteenth century, though certainly in less significant numbers.

Other than in metropolises like New York City, however, there have not been noncompensatory public schools. These schools cater to students who can succeed in conventional public institutions. There are also many nonpublic noncompensatory schools, though they have more of a historical tradition. Because they serve typical students, noncompensatory schools are more radical than compensatory schools, which may be viewed as last-ditch mechanisms to keep problem students in the system. It is when the student who gets good grades in P.S. 150 can enter an alternative school that the premises upon which public education is based are challenged.

Noncompensatory alternative schools like the East Hill Elementary school in Ithaca, New York and Palfrey Street School in Watertown, Massachusetts seem less concerned with preparing students for the future than with permitting them to pursue their own interests among an adult community vaguely committed to a new concept of society. Learning in compensatory schools like New York's Harlem Prep and Chicago's CAM Academy typically centers around training in the skills necessary for college admission and upward mobility. Learning in noncompensatory schools more closely resembles the traditional notion of a liberal education. Not unexpectedly, noncompensatory schools are populated primarily by middle class students. Their parents tend to be involved more in the operation of these schools than the working class and middle class parents of students in compensatory schools. Because most are boarding institutions, classical free schools are governed solely by students and teachers.

While both compensatory and noncompensatory alternative schools embody various innovations in curriculum, instructional methods, learning media, and evaluative techniques, more of the latter tend to involve new types of organization. Of the noncompensatory schools, the nonpublic schools are more radical organizationally than their public counterparts.

Money accounts for much of this variance. Compensatory schools are funded largely through government grants. These grants typically require some modified form of bureaucratic management, including directors and evaluators. Public noncompensatory schools are either financed by grants or regular tax monies. School districts generally require a relatively traditional organizational structure. Only in the nonpublic noncompensatory schools, most of which are tuition based, does adequate economic freedom exist to experiment with forms of governance.

The most radical of all new schools, the nonpublic noncompensatory alternative school is the least studied by professors of education and sociologists. A clear understanding of contemporary developments in education and in society at large requires the investigation not only of conventional public and private schools and of compensatory experiments, but also of new schools for students who are able to succeed in regular schools. Certainly the current popularity of voucher schemes and tuition credits indicates more than casual interest in noncompensatory alternative schools.

The Noncompensatory Public Alternative

Why are public school systems beginning to offer alternatives to their regular students? The answer may be deceptively simple. They have nothing to lose!

Public school systems are effective monopolies. They enjoy unchallenged control over tax monies. Whatever is needed to perpetuate this monopoly is done. In other words, public schools can accommodate numerous alternatives as long as the structure of public education remains intact. No alternative is acceptable, however, if it challenges the concept of bureaucracy.

The few public alternative schools that do embody radical structures are located either in communities like Berkeley and Ithaca—cities with somewhat homogeneous, university-based populations—or in such large metropolitan areas as New York and Philadelphia where desperation occasionally breeds real innovation. These exceptions tend to substantiate the view that parents and students usually do not have access to basic decision-making power. They enjoy the influence they have at the discretion of the public school bureaucracy. As the parents in Ocean Hill-Brownsville discovered, gaining influence downtown does not assure authority over teachers or principals. Clearly in education, as in industry, consumers have yet to gain control over production.

The nonpublic alternative represents a potential consumer revolution. Presently, though, it may be serving more as a mechanism to siphon off dissident parents and students. Providing this kind of service to local public schools is hardly revolutionary.

Despite these observations, both public and nonpublic noncompensatory alternative schools seem to embrace the spirit of community control and decentralization. Community control and decentralization may mean different things to different people depending on, among other things, their class status and the free time they have available for participation in school government. Community control varies according to the community's resources—financial, technical, temporal, and emotional. Lacking independent capital, working class parents who wish more of a voice in their children's education may be unable to do more than vote on budgets, bonds, and board members. Of course, the recent reaction against busing to achieve racial balance indicates that the power of the vote is not to be minimized. Still, that power is largely veto power. The vote is not suited to the implementation of new ideas or to daily involvement in educational decision making.

Parent involvement in school decision making appears more realistic in a nonpublic setting. To exist outside the public sphere, however, requires capital resources and prodigious effort. This may explain why nonpublic alternative schools are basically a middle class phenomenon. Middle class families have more money for tuition and more free time for participation.[28]

It is obvious that middle class families have the resources to permit involvement in alternative schools. Less apparent is the fact that middle class parents seem to have more of a desire to be involved than working class parents. Berger observes that education has become a latter day religion, providing an implicit set of judgments and guaranteeing salvation to the faithful learner.[29] As in traditional religious practice, the working class tends to be less questioning. Enjoying generally higher levels of education, middle class parents are prone to be more skeptical of sacred institutions. It would come as no surprise to find many of the young, middle class families involved in alternative schools to be areligious, members of underground churches or more radical sects like the Unitarians and the Friends.

Acknowledging that nonpublic alternative schools are primarily a middle class phenomenon does not explain why they emerged in the late sixties and early seventies rather than the forties or fifties. Community control and parent involvement are not new issues. Why have parents decided only recently to replace words with action?

A New Awareness?

What is there about the past decade that produced efforts to alter not only what schools teach and how they teach it, but also the way decisions are made and who makes the decisions? The previous section implies that rising affluence and increased free time, both class-based factors, explain why some are able to indulge a desire to work outside the system. But these factors do not explain why middle class parents want to revolutionize schooling in the first place.

The last ten years have marked a quiet revolution in the awareness of many persons. Young and college-educated individuals were forced to question why a country like the United States was involved in a war in Southeast Asia, and how it can tolerate poverty amidst abundance and excuse overt and covert discrimination and racism. In the past, social critics trained their sights on the functions of social institutions, not their structures. With the events of the sixties, it became clear to many that the real culprit might be bureaucratization. Too much distance had developed between the people and the agencies supposedly devoted to serving their needs.

When change-minded people began to organize marches, sit-ins, boycotts, and protest groups, they proved to themselves that complex cooperative efforts were possible without sacrificing democracy. If demonstrations and antiwar groups could be organized, why not alternative schools?

With the new awareness of how to organize and the importance of organizational structure came a level of sophistication that alienated some reformers. Kozol agonizes over Friedenberg's shift of focus from struggle for equal educational opportunity to "more sophisticated issues: 'institutional questions,' 'structural difficulties,' 'the analysis and function of the educational apparatus in and of itself'."[30] Why does a man like Friedenberg, an early *philosophe* of the new schools movement, alter his concerns from pedagogical change to the structure of schooling? Kozol may be mistaken to believe that Friedenberg, in a fit of esoteric delight, is losing touch with the real needs of disadvantaged students. What the popular sociologist seems to be saying is that there can be no realistic discussion of students' needs without first considering the structure of the schools dedicated ostensibly to the fulfillment of those needs. Considering that the free schools with which Kozol has been involved are parent-governed operations, it is likely that he too recognizes the importance of new decision-making structures.

The new awareness manifests itself in a thorough going critique of the way organizations like the public schools respond to the desires of those they supposedly serve. Black parents sensed some contradictions early. White parents' loss of control was less obvious. By the mid-sixties, however, it was apparent to many middle class persons that, as consumers, they had little control over production; as voters, they had little authority over the functioning of their government; and as parents, they had little voice in the operation of schools.

For some, the solution lay in decentralization, creating smaller and more responsive—though still representative—units of government. For others, only direct participation by all members of a community was acceptable. Some parents saw community control as a vehicle for sweeping social change, while others viewed increased involvement as a means of ironing out a few wrinkles in an otherwise suitable fabric.

Though generalizations invite exception, it can be argued that compensatory alternative schools, both public and nonpublic, serve to bolster the existing political and economic superstructure of this country. Parents supporting these schools tend to be working class and are involved less extensively in decision making than their middle class counterparts in noncompensatory alternative schools. The concern of working class parents is to open access to traditional routes to success, not to redefine success.

Parents supporting noncompensatory alternative schools include those who accept the existing society with some modifications. These parents might be concerned that artistic careers be accorded more acceptance in school or that young students be given some unscheduled time to play and explore. Open education, as derived in part from British infant schools, is the most coherent conceptualization of this kind of schooling.

Other parents, most of whom are found supporting nonpublic alternative schools, appear more radical and tend to reject the existing structure of American society as well as many of its operational values, notions of success, and life styles. At the same time, these parents often enjoy economic success and acceptance by the prevailing culture. The nonpublic noncompensatory alternative schools constitute a symbolic commune of sorts—an organization that permits parents of radical persuasion the luxury of dropping out and staying in. Despite efforts to attract black and disadvantaged students, these alternatives also represent the recognition by young, white middle class parents that their interests and values are not the same as those who remain in public schools— namely, minority and working class students. There is little rhetoric, as in the progressive education movement, designed to persuade all parents that alternative schooling is the answer. There is a quiet acceptance of the fact that white middle class families have their own thing to do.

The thing the young, white middle class feels compelled to do is develop real, functioning communities of interest. Too often stranded in suburbs or cities, they find themselves surrounded by persons from different backgrounds and with opposing values. Feelings of isolation and alienation arise. All classes of people are subject to these feelings, but the working class and older middle America types possess organizations that offer affiliation and the promise of group solidarity—in other words, community. Whether at the local union hall, church, or ethnic club, the average American can readily find companionship and moral support. Young middle class parents of liberal to radical political persuasion, however, tend to reject these kinds of organizations. The nonpublic alternative school may represent one of the few acceptable antidotes to their social isolation. Others include food co-ops, communes, underground churches, and encounter groups.

Conclusions

The fact that some parents view the alternative school as a vehicle for social change is, in many respects, unfortunate. Bereiter is the most recent educationist to argue that the school may not be suited to perform a variety of socially-relevant tasks.[31] Cremin criticizes progressive educators for taking too seriously the demands of citizens that schools adopt functions handled traditionally by the family and other agencies.[32] Ylvisaker credits sociologist James Coleman with the following admonition: "Don't expect schools to work on their own. They can reinforce the values of the culture around them. But, where those values are negative, schools can do little to soften the tragic consequences."[33] The school—public or nonpublic, alternative or conventional, elementary or secondary, compensatory or noncompensatory—reflects an existing culture through the behaviors it sanctions and the organizational structure it adopts.

As long as radical social critics and counterculturists expect the alternative school to be the bellwether of social change, they will be disappointed. Schools do not create new values or ideologies. They transmit existing ones. When no clear-cut system of beliefs exists, the school's task is virtually impossible. It is no surprise that many alternative schools fail as a result of ideological squabbles over false issues like structure versus nonstructure, or shaping the student versus freeing the student. These are false issues because no situation is devoid of structure and no student is completely free. To belabor such questions and to avoid constructing a coherent system of fundamental beliefs, assure that an alternative school will do little more than reflect the confusion and existing operational values of contemporary society.

That the school as an organization is not suited to occupy the vanguard of revolution is seen in the experience of countries like China. Social change resulted from the establishment of alternative political, economic, and military organizations, not new schools. Through these alternatives, a radical system of beliefs becomes clarified and incorporated into an ideology. In turn, the ideology guided the functioning of the schools.

Recent movements for social change in the United States have generally lacked alternative economic and political organizations. Conceivably communes, cooperatives, and collectives constitute potentially radical agencies. Without these kinds of organizations, it is naive to think that alternative schools will have any lasting impact on society (though they may well influence existing schools). Etzioni discusses this problem:

The contention that personal growth and societal changes are much harder to come by than we had assumed, especially via one version or another of the educationalist-enlightenment approach, is not a joyful message, but one whose full implications we must learn to accept before we can devise more effective social programs. Once we cease turning to ads, leaflets, counselors, or teachers for salvation, we may realize that more can be achieved by engineers, doctors, social movements, and public-interest groups; and the educators will find new and much-needed allies.[34]

Without these allies, the educator can accomplish very little. A school can command the commitment of a family only as long as there are children of the right age to attend. In other words, a school does not provide the potential for continuous contact and consciousness-raising for any given member. As an organization, it cannot participate in any effort to change society without its own society to reinforce the appropriate behavior and discourage the inappropriate.

Most radical alternative schools are located in cities and suburbs where new behaviors cannot be rewarded consistently. Ironically, the type of alternative school most suited to nurture a new society is the classical or Summerhillian free school—also the type least willing to socialize students according to any given ideology or set of values.

The discussion of radical alternatives does imply that a new wave of radical ferment has struck the United States. The election of 1972, however, must not be forgotten. A majority of Americans are apparently satisfied with the status quo. The quest for community control may be little more than a sentimental longing for influence in a society run increasingly by experts.[35] The interest in freeing students and stimulating individuality may be as much a resurgence of libertarianism as a precursor of radical change.

History provides few clues. An argument can be advanced that radicalized individuals emerge only from societies that are basically radical. Conversely, one can argue that a radical society cannot exist without first having a nucleus of radicalized members. The first argument would find little promise of basic change in the United States of the early seventies. The second argument is more optimistic.

In any event, the seeming inability of persons engaged in alternative schools to fashion a clear ideology of social change may reflect simply an unwillingness to do so. Parents accept public pronouncement on the need for change, but they may be satisfied privately with the comfort and security of middle class living. Or, they may be dissatisfied, but unimpressed by the existing alternatives. There are still too few people involved in alternative schools to determine whether they represent broad-based discontent, a new front for youthful protest, an outlet for bored intellectuals, a focus for New Left activities, a new level of generation gap rejectionism, or all of these.

Although alternative schools continue to form, the attrition rate is high. There are numerous reasons for closing these schools: lack of funds, exhaustion of teachers and parents, ideological schisms, pressure from local authorities, and lack of student interest. In most cases, these factors are surmountable, given the appropriate motivation and energy. The fact that alternative schools close, however, may not indicate failure so much as fulfillment. It is typical to think of a school as an immortal organization outliving any one group of students. In fact, the alternative school may be a new type of organization dubbed by some as a "temporary organization."[36]

The temporary organization, or ad-hocracy as Toffler describes it, is an organization acknowledged to have a nonperpetual existence and a relatively limited purpose. Conceivably the need for community or for influence in decision making is not continuous. A year or two's experience establishing and supporting an alternative school may satisfy a parent's desire for affiliation and a student's interest in open exploration. Alternative schools affect families differently. Some return to public schools with a new-found respect for formalized learning and bureaucratic management. Others leave one alternative school to join another. These persons utilize the alternative school as a point of entry into a new culture or life style.

Whatever the effect of the alternative school experience on those involved, it is certainly more meaningful and intensive for the individuals responsible for the actual creation of the school. Families joining late often feel like outsiders. The establishment of an alternative school may well be a more significant learning experience than anything that occurs subsequently.

Once established, an alternative school can become as routine and unchallenging as a conventional school to many parents, teachers, and students. As organizations, schools also have a time-bound quality not found among many economic, political, social, or religious bodies. Students grow older and leave school. Few parents are willing to extend their commitment to an alternative school beyond their offspring's graduation. The high turnover rate among families alone can act as a powerful counterforce to the generation of a permanent sense of community. It is difficult for a parent to establish lasting affiliations knowing that in a few years he and his child will not be involved in the school.

Ultimately, community springs from productive endeavors rather than reflective efforts. Learning is generally too individualistic an activity to stimulate group cohesion. Living and working together are better suited to social change. Developments in the therapeutic treatment of drug abusers are instructive. Successes recorded in the rehabilitation of addicts have come about as a result of involvement in total living situations such as Synanon and Phoenix House, rather than through drug education programs, outpatient service, or chemotherapy. In these organizations, members live, work, *and* learn together, thus providing the consistent reinforcement necessary to alter life styles.

Most alternative schools symbolize a reaction to outmoded, inhumane, unresponsive educational practice. Some new schools also represent a concerted effort for social change. Evidence of the foregoing is not to be found in the rhetoric or public ideologies surrounding such ventures. These statements too often concern philosophical issues in learning theory. Neither is such evidence found in a new black studies curriculum, a program of individualized instruction, or a classroom filled with gerbils, terraria, and play dough. The desire for social change is revealed in new roles for parents, teachers, and students and in different decision-making processes. I concur with those who believe that the nature of a society cannot be separated from the structure of that society's institutions.

7 Critical Issues

Donald A. Myers

Five major issues confronting open education are discussed in this chapter: (1) lack of definition, (2) problems of adoption, (3) inadequate attention to curriculum, (4) difficulties associated with teachers' ability to implement, and (5) resistance of parents and appropriateness of open education for children from lower socioeconomic class homes.

Definition

The most significant problem encountered in studying open education is its lack of definition. Open education has several meanings depending upon which author one reads. The problem of definition extends to the so-called free school movement as well. Marin attended a conference on free schools and noted that "none of the speakers bothered to define the roots and aims of free schools. I don't know whether they simply take their objectives for granted or have forgotten them."[1]

Some principals and teachers have been willing to adopt open education even though it has not been defined. Indeed, many professors of education present open education to their students like evangelists rather than scholars. Some members of the research community, however, have been at work attempting to conceptualize and define open education. The most useful investigations have come from two prestigious independent research organizations that began to conceptualize open education in the late sixties and early seventies.

The Stanford Research Institute undertook a study with Vivian S. Sherman as consultant. She began with the belief that schools appear to be suffering from a severe case of overstructuring in some of their major components. She felt also that there is a tendency toward rigidity at the very time when there is a comprehensive need for greater openness and flexibility to create a desirable future and to prevent the occurrence of a dismal one. Thus, she began with a decided and admitted bias against the existing structured school.

Her overall conceptualization is explained in Figure 7-1. She described two educational alternatives—structured and openness—identifying values, assumptions, and latent dangers of each. Briefly, her overall description of both models is as follows:

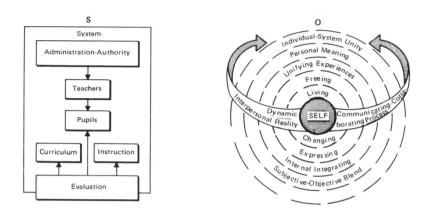

Classroom is place where planned instructional events occur.

Focus is primarily upon what is done to and for prospective learners, i.e., method, materials, grouping arrangements, teacher-pupil ratio, physical resources and facilities.

Attention is primarily given to verbal interactions associated with instructional approach, e.g., direct vs indirect, climate in which instruction takes place.

Individual differences receive attention primarily in relation to response of different groups to different methods or approaches.

Educator effectiveness is in terms of success achieved in raising IQ points, teaching basic skills and knowledge, i.e., carrying out formal role.

Assessment is primarily of pupil growth in academic achievement deemed important to broader culture.

Little direct focus upon system as a whole or educators as people.

Classroom is a dynamic social system and a microlab of larger milieu.

Focus is upon transactions that occur within the environment and in relation to those events which impinge from outside of it.

Feedback is continuous and emits from and impinges upon all participants.

Qualities and characteristics of participants are vital ingredients.

Main focus is upon interpersonal communication, especially nonverbal cues related to expectancies and self-fulfilling prophecies; search is directed to subtle variables traditionally not considered part of the field.

Human and physical resources are seen as stimulants for transacting and are examined for potential influence upon learner selectivity and their release and regulating effects.

Critical questions involve optimal stimulation for growth without disrupting security to point of debilitation.

Connections between internal and external realities are important concerns.

Figure 7-1. "Alternative Conceptions of Process Variables." Source: Vivian S. Sherman, *Two Contrasting Educational Models: Applications and Policy Implications* (Menlo Park, Calif.: Stanford Research Institute, 1970), p. 45.

Alternative S, the structured situation, stands for security and sureness gained through the equating of system and structure—through organization which preserves the status quo. This is the world of order, pre-arrangement, externality, and objectivity. It seeks to prepare for the future by conserving the past, by inculcating the young with what is known, needed, and commonly valued. Its primary focus is upon important segments of accumulated knowledge, core beliefs, and skills required for success in the culture. Continuity, conservation, and societal fit are predominant concerns. Formal socialization agents are trained and certified to accomplish these ends; they are hired, judged, and retained on the basis of their willingness to assume this responsibility, of how neatly they fit the system, and of how adequately their charges acquire generally valued meanings and skills. Control and power are exerted through external regulation or position in the system.[2]

Alternative O, openness, stands for ongoingness, and opportune moments for growth. This is the alive and dynamic world of movement and flow, a world tuned to the internal, subjective, immediate, and felt. Meaning is personal and comes out of present experiencing and conceptualizing. The future is constantly in the process of becoming; changingness is ever present. Continuity lies in awareness of constancy in direction, manner of unfolding, or in growing appreciations, deepening understandings, and strengthening of self. Uniqueness, expansion of human limits from within, and coping power are basic concerns. Adults are models of individuality, creative adaptability, and self-transcendence who relate to and grow along with the young. Together they test and push outward the boundaries of sensing, feeling, thinking, doing, and expressing. Joint endeavors broaden the power and internal control that is felt within each person.[3]

Sherman's conceptualization describes models at extreme ends of a continuum. *Alternative S* is Platonic and instrumental. *Alternative O* is Rousseauian and naturalistic. Such dichotomies can be useful to those who wish to propose more moderate and realistic educational alternatives, as neither model Sherman proposes has been, nor hopefully ever will be, fully realized in the United States. *Alternative S*, for example, implies that *Alternative O* is without structure. Many groups of parents and teachers have labored to resolve the structure/no structure problem. Unfortunately, they ignore the fact that a structureless situation is impossible. In the absence of a planned, explicit routine, a "structure by default" occurs and school activities become determined by hidden factors such as the peer group, adult ego-involvement, and group dynamics.[4] Thus, models like the ones Sherman offers must be regarded with caution. Taken at face value, *Alternative S* is an insult to man; *Alternative O*, an insult to mankind.

At the same time Sherman was developing her models, four investigators from Educational Development Corporation were also attempting to conceptualize open education.[5] They proposed a two-dimension conceptual scheme as shown in Figure 7-2.

The scheme is unusual in that it includes both the teacher and the child rather than the more common practice of developing different models for each. Thus, the vertical axis seeks to determine the degree of choice and freedom of

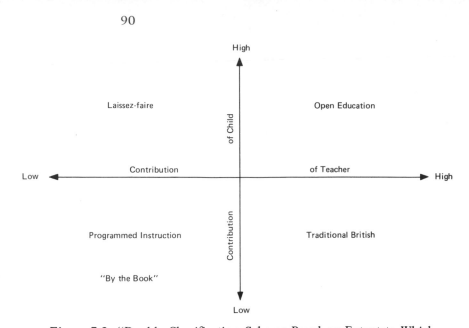

Figure 7-2. "Double Classification Scheme Based on Extent to Which (1) the Individual Teacher and (2) the Individual Child *Is an Active Contributor* to Decisions Regarding the Content and Process of Learning." Source: Anne M. Bussis and Edward A. Chittenden, *Analysis of an Approach to Open Education* (Princeton, New Jersey: Educational Testing Service, 1970), p. 23.

children. The horizontal axis seeks to determine the degree of contribution or involvement of teachers in children's learning.

The investigators at EDC maintain that the most useful educational classrooms or environments are high on both axes, thus the upper right-hand quadrant "open education." The lower left-hand quadrant is rated low on both axes and thus antithetical to open education. In this quadrant, "programmed instruction," the child's contribution to his own learning is minimal. His views concerning the programed material may be sought, but there is little emphasis on student choice. Similarly, the teacher's contribution is minimal as he is subservient to the programed materials being used by children. While a competent teacher will know the content of the program to assist children with problems, many programed materials are so thoroughly sequenced that a child should not encounter difficulties that require the aid of a teacher.

The lower left-hand quadrant is the most distant from an open classroom . . . the teacher here is a passive conveyor of decisions made elsewhere; and unlike the

upper left, the children have very little freedom or chance to express themselves. . . . these are the rooms where education is seen as a grim business, a
preparation for life, rather than life itself.[6]

The right-hand quadrant, "traditional British," can be labeled just as accurately "traditional American." In this quadrant, the teacher is quite evident. It is
his responsibility to bring the curriculum to children. Lecturing is common as
the teacher and his instructional materials are the purveyors of ideas. Textbooks
and workbooks are usually in evidence. The child is given some choices of
activities, but these choices are highly regulated. Some part of the week may be
set aside for children to do their own thing, but this time is normally restricted
and is seen as an appendix to the academic program which is viewed as more
important.

Children have little say about what they will do. . . . [The teacher] . . . may be
very active in diagnosis, making it her business to find out how the children are
progressing. . . . They give a great deal of thought to what goes on in their room
and perhaps as to how they are reaching each pupil. On the other hand, they give
little credit or chance for decision making to students, preferring to think of
themselves in the starring role and occupying "center stage" of the classroom.[7]

The upper-left quadrant, "laissez-faire," can be viewed as significantly
different from both the right- and left-hand quadrants. The child has considerable choice of alternatives. The most extreme example of a school in this
quadrant would be Summerhill, but some private alternative or free schools fit
this pattern. The teacher makes little contribution in the laissez-faire environment and usually only when responding to a student's request for assistance.

The adult plays a very supportive but entirely nondirective role, the children
having great freedom which occasionally erupts in chaos. . . . The preschool
teacher here is likely to be a rather bland individual who does not come through
very strongly as a person. . . . But she is servant more than teacher, the emphasis
is on nurturance rather than education.[8]

While this conceptual scheme is very useful, its principal value is its use in
"assessing change in classrooms."[9]   While it is not intended as, and is not, a
definition of open education, it constitutes a definition in the sense that it offers
a schematic model that distinguishes open education from other models of
education.

This scheme must be viewed with as much caution as Sherman's. The authors
may be guilty of creating a tautology in which good education is none other
than open education. If open education is conceived to be the only alternative, it
is doubtful that it will ever be a manageable, clear concept or set of practices.

Aside from the above mentioned studies, several independent investigators have been at work attempting to define open education. Earlier efforts include studies by Barth[10] and Rathbone.[11] The most thorough attempt to date has been made by Walberg and Thomas, who used the previous authors' works plus those of sixteen other informed writers to develop eight distinct themes in open education. The themes are paraphrased as follows:

1. *Provisioning for Learning*—Manipulative materials are supplied in great diversity and range. Children have free movement about the classroom. Talking is encouraged. No norm grouping.
2. *Humaneness, Respect, Openness, and Warmth*—Use of student-made material. Students discipline themselves. Many student-made products around the room.
3. *Diagnosis of Learning Events*—Students correct their own work. Teacher observes and asks.
4. *Instruction*—Individualized. No texts or workbooks.
5. *Evaluation*—Teacher takes notes. Individualized. Few tests.
6. *Seeking Opportunities for Professional Growth*—Teacher uses the assistance of someone else. Teacher works with colleague.
7. *Self-Perception of Teacher*—Teacher tries to keep all children within sight so that she can make sure they are doing what they are supposed to do.
8. *Assumptions about Children and Learning Process*—Classroom climate warm and accepting. Student seen as important.[12]

Walberg and Thomas assert that the scale developed clearly distinguishes open from traditional classes. "Open classes differ sharply from Traditional on 5 of 8 criteria—Provisioning, Humaneness, Diagnosis, Instruction, and Evaluation."[13]

Another study related to defining open education was conducted by Tuchman, Cochran, and Travers. They sought to assess the extent to which open education classrooms differed from controlled classrooms with respect to teaching process—the behavior of teachers; and teaching product—the outcomes of students. So far as teaching process, open education classrooms in grades 1-3 scored significantly higher in only three of twenty-three categories. In grades 4-5, significant differences occurred in only five of twenty-three categories. The differences between open and traditional classrooms seemed to center largely around the method of organizing the children (small vs. large groups) which produced high scores in flexible use of space, teacher responding, and teacher warmth and acceptance.[14]

So far as teaching product, the authors conclude that "these new patterns do not seem to affect achievement but they do seem to cause students to like school more."[15] In this regard, I am reminded of the remark of a colleague that if the aim of schooling were to produce children who like school, he could do so with much less money than is presently being spent.

The results of most studies to date have been fairly predictable. Unfortunately, they have not been too useful in defining open education or the characteristics of open education teachers. The methodological problems, while simple to identify, virtually defy solution. Similarly, Walberg and Thomas assert that open education is antithetical to those "who classify the curriculum into subjects, group learners by ability, and view knowledge as represented authoritatively by the teacher as in prescribed vicarious methods of instruction."[16]

In simple words, MacDonald and Walberg and Thomas suggest that traditional classrooms have a static curriculum, a controlling teacher, didactic instruction with accompanying textbooks, workbooks, etc. Open classrooms have a flexible curriculum, a receptive teacher, an emphasis on process learning with accompanying multiple instructional materials. The problem is that once a researcher assumes such a position, any study contrasting traditional and open classrooms is superfluous as the results are virtually inescapable.

While Walberg and Thomas used a thorough research design, the manner in which they identified traditional classes is subject to question. Trainees, for example, completed the observation rating scale after viewing a mathematics project training film in which an exceptional teacher instructed an eager class using a traditional lesson format.[17] What is a traditional lesson format?

It is questionable that a concept such as open education should be advocated before it has been defined. To confound educators further, Sarason, et al., suggest that "*even* if our basic conceptions were correct, there was the possibility that we would implement them erroneously because of our own imperfections as individuals."[18] (My italics) Open education suffers from a lack of definition and, as will be noted later, is dependent upon highly skilled teachers for implementation.

Researchers will continue to have great difficulty defining open education as a discrete concept. It will likely remain a multidimensional ideology. It appears that educators in the United States have collected under the label of open education a number of "best existing practices" and imbued them with the aura of an ideology, or as Walberg and Thomas state, "a related set of ideas and methods."[19] Barth supports this position when he asserts that "informal classrooms must become synonymous with the best educational experiences for children."[20]

There is one advantage in proposing a concept that defies definition. Without a definition, evaluation is impossible. The lack of evaluation represents security for teachers. Is the ultimate mark of open education productive or simply happy children? The absence of a definition with accompanying criteria allows the practicing open education teacher to *escape assessment*. Without assessment and evaluation, moreover, it is uncertain whether open education can or should have a lasting effect on public schooling.

Finally, it should be acknowledged that open education proponents may not be so uninformed as they seem. It may be that they know open education cannot be defined. Thus, they choose what they like about primary schooling, give the product credibility through the use of unassailable labels such as open, contend that it is working in British schools, maintain that it is a fairly discrete entity, and accuse those who oppose it as inhumane, structured, and the most dreaded label of all, "traditional."[21] This explanation at least makes the last few years of frantic activity more understandable.

Adoption

It is not likely that open education will be adopted widely in the United States because several factors will serve to undermine the efforts of its proponents; namely, (1) the tendency of educators to adopt an innovation without careful thought; (2) the tendency of educators to adopt an innovation without changing the educational program; (3) the tendency of educators to adopt an innovation and misinterpret it; (4) the difficulty of implementing a multidimensional innovation; (5) the difficulty of implementing any new form of organization.

Bandwagon Phenomenon

One of the perplexing phenomena in American education is the eagerness of many eduators to adopt an innovation for which there is no clear definition and about which there is limited knowledge from research. This is the bandwagon phenomenon.

Some educators are disposed to search for the new, the different, the flashy, the radical, or the revolutionary. Once an idea or practice, such as "team teaching," "nongrading," and (more recently) "differential staffing" and "performance contracting," has been so labeled by the Establishment, many teachers and administrators are quick to adopt it.[22]

Sarason, et al., warn, as have countless others, that "before you start shaping the future you had better know and deal with the past."[23] As Leese's chapter makes clear, most persons in education have little knowledge of the historical antecedents of open education.

Open education is not only accepted uncritically, but it is also advocated for all children regardless of academic level, mental deficiency, race, socioeconomic level, or degree of motivation. If the medical profession used such an approach, the president of the American Medical Association would advocate the use of a new drug for all patients regardless of sex, age, weight, medical history, or indeed type of illness. Furthermore, he would take to rostrums at medical conventions and advocate the new drug before it had been tested, or if it had been tested but shown to have no significant difference.

The tendency for educators to jump on the bandwagon has been noted before, but there is little research to explain this phenomenon. Some persons have offered the plausible explanation that administrators at all levels who wish to promote their careers and make a name for themselves are wise to be innovative even if the innovation proves to be undesirable. Such administrators are viewed as effective because they take risks, a desirable characteristic for executives. But this does not appear to be an adequate explanation. Thus far, the adoption of open education seems to be due to the tendency of educators to adopt anything that promises to salvage an institution that is under severe attack by citizens, legislators, students, and teachers themselves—a general dissatisfaction with the status quo and the belief that nothing can be worse.

Adopt and Remain the Same

An intriguing peculiarity in education is the tendency to adopt innovations without changing the educational program. This parallels Sarason's conclusion that the more things change, the more they remain the same.[24] In the study reported by Myers and Duke in Chapter 5, they encountered persons in several schools who professed to have adopted open education, but who had no evidence to support such a claim. This phenomenon is not new in education.

In the sixties, the nongraded school was popularized. Within a decade, almost every forward-looking school was nongraded. Yet, when persons write authorities for a list of nongraded schools, they respond normally with a letter to the effect that they do not know of any.

A similar phenomenon exists in team teaching. Schools claim to be teaming, but it is difficult to find "real" teams in operation. Everyone is teaming who says he is teaming because definitions to date have been so general.

The idea that an educational innovation can be adopted in a school without altering the educational program seems paradoxical, but it makes sense if (1) persons in the school have little knowledge of the innovation and are thus unable to implement it, or (2) the innovation being adopted is not a concept but only a phrase or ideology that in fact does not exist. So far as open education is concerned, both explanations come uncomfortably close to being true. Many teachers know very little about open education and are thus unable to modify their behavior to correspond with what might be considered open. Teachers cannot behave in an "open" manner because open education has not been well defined to date. Thus, we can expect schools to seemingly adopt open education without substantially altering their educational programs.

Adopt and Misinterpret

It was first stated that educators have a tendency to adopt an innovation early and uncritically—the bandwagon phenomenon. Second, it was stated that educators adopt an innovation without changing the educational program. There remains an additional factor that rounds out this triad regarding adoption—the tendency for educators to seemingly adopt an innovation but to misinterpret it.

Schoolmen did such a poor job implementing progressive education earlier in the century that Dewey was forced late in his career to write *Experience and Education* to correct the misconceptions of his followers. Similarly, Goodlad spent much of his time in the early sixties advocating nongradedness and much of his time in the late sixties trying to convince persons that what they were doing was not nongrading. Barth notes that "educators are quick to assimilate new ideas into their cognitive and operational framework. But in so doing they often distort the original conception without recognizing either the distortion or the assumptions violated by the distortion."[25]

The major reason for misinterpretation would seem to be that the concept being advanced is so highly complex that mistakes are bound to be made by persons attempting to implement it. Undoubtedly, there is some truth to this assertion. Another reason, however, may be that the innovation is not well defined, thus making adoption difficult because teachers do not know what to do.

This explanation seems especially plausible in the three innovations mentioned—nongradedness, team teaching, and open education. Numerous books and articles have been written about nongradedness, but there is still uncertainty whether to classify it as a philosophy, a method of organization, or both. While the nongraded school was advocated widely in the early sixties, it was not until 1967 that a doctoral dissertation was written to identify the distinguishing characteristics of a nongraded school, i.e., to provide a definition.[26]

So far as team teaching is concerned, over five hundred references were cited in *Educational Index* between 1960 and 1970, but the concept still lacks a definition unless one accepts the initial definition offered by Shaplin which is thought not to be sufficiently discriminating.[27] Anderson, perhaps the leading proponent of team teaching today, refuses to define it. He suggests instead that a "team" may be a team by determining the degree to which it meets seven *illustrative* (not definitive) criteria.[28]

Open education suffers from the lack of a definition as did team teaching and nongradedness previously. This analysis is not meant to suggest that open education should be abandoned. It does suggest, however, that it is extremely difficult to implement it accurately and that misinterpretations are bound to be made because the concept is so poorly defined. Johnson noted in the opening chapter that it cannot be assumed that when an idea goes awry in practice, the fault lies in the indiscretion, insincerity, and, I would add, incompetence of its practitioners. The idea *itself* may have serious shortcomings. He quotes Crawford as follows: "An inadequate theory of what you are doing is bound to let you down even though your practice may in some measure remedy the defects in your theory."[29] This analysis, to the degree it is valid, clearly *shifts the "blame" for misinterpretation of a concept* from the implementor (teacher) to the initiator (scholar) or to a lack of capable interpreters of scholars' work.

If Dewey and his contemporaries had defined progressive education more accurately in the first place, Dewey may not have needed to write *Experience and Education.* Similarly, if Weber, Rogers, Kohl, *et al.*, spent more time defining open education rather than extolling its seemingly endless virtues, teachers would not now be misinterpreting open space, team teaching, contracts, use of corridors, nongrading, increased freedom of choice for children, etc., as open education.

Multidimensionality

Open education is multidimensional. It is pervasive in the strict sense of the word and thus accompanied by more unanticipated events. Smith and Keith observe: "The more outcomes that are unanticipated, the greater the need for additional resources both to implement the program and to respond to the increased variety introduced by the unintended events."[30] They suggest a step-by-step, gradual shift that would temper this chain of events.

In 1966, Etzioni wrote an essay entitled, "A Gradualist Strategy at Work." His analysis included nine generalizations concerning innovations, two of which are especially pertinent to open education. He suggested (1) amplifying the close and underplaying the remote; (2) phasing of adjustment—making all the changes, adjustments, and sacrifices into many small and almost insignificant steps.[31]

Concerning his first generalization, teachers in some schools engaged in open education evidence a tiresome concern about the remote. This is not necessarily undesirable, but it has some negative consequences. Some teachers find it necessary to meet in the evenings to explore the philosophy of open education. I was consultant to a group of teachers in a private school experimenting with open education. I was asked to attend an evening session concerning the philosophy of open education. I attended but suggested that the time might be better spent discussing how to individualize the reading program. My advice was ignored and the teachers stayed up until 2:10 A.M. on a school night, talking about the philosophy of open education. They adjourned tired, confused, and generally intoxicated. The scene would be analogous to the Joint Chiefs of Staff discussing the philosophy of war the evening before the invasion of Normandy. At the time, the school was in almost complete disorganization, a fact which the teachers apparently found necessary to ignore.

Concerning Etzioni's second generalization, it was noted that teachers often were attempting to change many, if not all, dimensions of the school simultaneously. A wiser practice might have been to take the advice of an English headmistress, "run a free day when you and your children *can*."[32] (Italics in the original) If Etzioni's generalization is valid, attempting to change many dimensions will not likely succeed. He would argue for breaking down open education into subunits and attacking them one at a time. But many teachers are "true believers"[33] who have little patience with improving one aspect of the classroom at a time.

Orlosky and Smith studied sixty-three major educational changes attempted during the past seventy-five years. They indicated the degree to which the innovations were put into effect and noted the factors that contributed to their success or failure. They suggested that the weight of the cognitive burden is a significant factor regarding permanent change. "If the cognitive load is light, i.e., if not many people are required to learn many new facts and procedures, a change is more likely to persist than if the burden is heavy."[34] The multifaceted nature of open education makes it seem unlikely that it will result in permanent change.

New Organization

Many persons who wish to see open education adopted more widely in America do not understand sufficiently the nature of organizations per se. The following statement is representative of the types of concerns voiced by authors knowledgeable about organizations:

Time and again we have observed in the creation of new settings the almost complete lack of self-conscious effort to be aware of the tendencies towards organizational craziness, and, therefore, to develop vehicles for sensing and controlling them. . . . The aim is not to avoid conflict or controversy, but to recognize, surface, and resolve it. Missionary zeal of leaders, exhortations and inspirational sermons, and crystal-clear organizational charts describing functions and responsibilities are either inadequate or worthless.[35]

In addition to these types of problems, open education is burdened with the fact that it is supposedly different from the educational programs it purports to replace. It is viewed as a new type of organization. As Duke observes in Chapter 6, public school bureaucracies seem willing to tolerate any type of change except organizational change. Curriculum, instructional methods, evaluative techniques all are open to alteration, but schools have rarely submitted to basic changes in decision-making processes or role definitions. In analyzing organizations, Stinchcombe suggests four factors that may be significant generalizations when applied to open education:

(a) New organizations, especially new types of organizations, generally involve new roles, which have to be learned.
(b) The process of inventing new roles, the determination of their mutual relations and of structuring the fields of rewards and sanctions so as to get maximum performance, have high costs in time, worry, conflict, and temporary inefficiency.

(c) New organizations must rely heavily on social relations among strangers. This means that relations of trust are much more precarious in new than old organizations. . . .

(d) One of the main resources of old organizations is a set of stable ties to those who use organizational services.[36]

If forming a new organization is as complex as Stinchcombe suggests, it is little wonder why teachers have to work so hard and why programs have not developed to their potential as soon as their proponents expect. Few school districts, in fact, provide time off for teachers in open education classrooms to cope with the new organizational structure. Unless considerable released time is provided, it would be foolish to believe that open education will be widely adopted or, where "adopted," be any different from the program it supposedly replaces.

Curriculum

It is an understatement to assert that curriculum is not a science. Regardless of its status in the community of disciplines and subdisciplines, there is such a thing as curriculum and it is hazardous to ignore it.

I shall not state *a* definition of curriculum for fear the reader will take exception to it rather than concentrate on the issue I wish to emphasize; namely, that the lack of an understanding of curriculum may be a central weakness of open education.

I have identified three problems related to curriculum that cause confusion: (1) objectives, (2) continuity and sequence, and (3) integration.

Objectives

Curriculum is anticipatory to or a priori to instruction. Curriculum involves objectives, intended learning outcomes for children, or whatever term a particular author wishes to use. Authors such as Sherman,[37] Kohl,[38] and Barth[39] view curriculum, if defined in terms of anticipated learning outcomes for children, as either immoral or superfluous. Those who view it as immoral believe children should not be told what to do by adults. This is instrumental, preparing children for a future life but not for the present. Those who view it as superfluous believe children capable of charting their own way through schooling.

Are objectives immoral or superfluous? Quite the contrary. For example, some children are socially and emotionally withdrawn. I maintain such children should be strongly encouraged to become more secure, outgoing, and gregarious with peers and adults. A competent teacher can think of many learning experiences to assist such children. But as soon as the teacher intercedes with a learning experience, he is imposing his or society's values upon the child who presumably is content being withdrawn. I can think of few things more immoral than for a parent or teacher to sit idly by, like an unobtrusive valet, while a child slips further and further into a protective shell caused by a home environment that is perhaps too protective or threatening. We have all seen such children in intermediate and senior high schools and can only lament that they have grown to that age without a more confident and outgoing attitude toward themselves and life. The same line of reasoning can be applied to children who need assistance in reading, writing, mathematics, physical education, art, music, and a variety of other worthwhile activities deemed significant by a vast majority of adults. "George Denison, who asks what is so precious about a curriculum, says that when he decided José was ready to read, and José refused to do so, he gave José lessons in reading, and José learned to read. This is having a curriculum in mind, if not in the catalogue."[40]

I am not arguing for a rigid schedule of activities for children nor for uncompromising teachers who demand instant obedience and progress in all areas. I support the team of teachers in Los Angeles who permitted a five-year-old girl to lie in a large sandbox with limbs outstretched for three hours several days without insisting the child do something else or even questioning the child's actions. I would criticize these teachers, however, if they permitted such a practice to continue over a week without some plan for determining the reasons for such behavior.

The resistance to objectives is often accompanied by a resistance to knowledge per se. Barth notes that one person cannot determine what a child should learn and that there is no way to predict and plan what knowledge the teacher must have.[41] Two proponents of process learning make the astonishing assertion that "knowledge keeps no better than fish."[42] If such were the case, one wonders why the authors bothered to write a monograph, as the time for production certainly exceeded six months and their very assertions would smell like fish by the time their manuscript was in print. In this instance their assertion inadvertently supports their point. Fortunately, however, the statement was not correct in the first place.

Regarding this point of view, one can only wonder at the response that would be made by such persons as Aristotle, Darwin, Mme. Curie, and hundreds of other scholars in the history of mankind who have spent their lives in an attempt to push back the frontiers of ignorance. Darwin's theory of evolution has been modified; there is no universal agreement on Hamlet's problem; Billy Budd remains an enigma. But to maintain that the knowledge these scientists and authors have generated keeps no better than fish is more than an exaggeration. It is simply inane. "Young people must be qualified to deal with ideas not yet born and with discoveries not yet made,"[43] but responsible parents and teachers have a "sacred" and "moral" commitment to transmit what they consider relevant and "definitive" knowledge to the young (including, but not exclusively, process learning) until such time as complete disorganization or stagnation exist in our society.

In actual fact, there is much more rhetoric than genuine disagreement concerning the lack of need for objectives with accompanying wider student choices. Open education offers the child limited choice as to what he learns, although there is a growing sympathy among teachers that children should be permitted increased freedom to explore objectives of their own, provided they are not inconsistent with societal values.

Continuity and Sequence

Continuity and sequence are as much a part of curriculum as torts and contracts in the practice of law. The standard definition was offered by Tyler over two decades ago:

Continuity refers to the vertical reiteration of major curriculum elements. . . . it is necessary to see that there is recurring and continuing opportunity for these skills to be practiced and developed. Sequence is related to continuity but goes beyond it. . . . Sequence as a criterion emphasizes the importance of having each successive experience build upon the preceding one but to go more broadly and deeply into the matters involved.[44]

The need for sequence should be apparent to anyone interested in learning efficiency. It would be inefficient if a teacher placed "Othello" or "Long Day's Journey into Night" on the reading table in a classroom composed of young children. While all teachers would agree, many persons persist in the belief that continuity and sequence are somehow antithetical to open education. In truth, continuity and sequence are essential to open education as they are necessary for the individualization of instruction. One can emphasize the necessity for continuity and sequence without disparaging the need for children to have some time for free and inefficient learning. It has been asserted that some programed materials and computer programs are so tightly sequenced that children become bored and even alienated by the "dehumanized" approach. This is true, but this simply suggests a modification of the program, not a rejection of continuity and sequence. The continuity and sequence of learning experiences are necessary for all children with or without programed material or computer instruction.

Integration

Tyler notes that integration refers to the horizontal relationship of curriculum experiences. "The organization of these experiences should be such that they help the student increasingly to get a unified view and to unify his behavior in relation to the elements dealt with."[45] Tyler's initial conception of integration was elaborated upon considerably by Dressel in the 1958 *NSSE Yearbook*.[46] For my purpose, however, Tyler's definition will suffice.

Many proponents of open education wisely cite the need for integration although some apparently believe it cannot be done for children. Integration is not only more efficient, since it tends to reduce duplication, but it is more meaningful to children because it often involves the combining of disciplines to help them understand the problems they confront.

While integration is "theoretically" desirable, it is an ideal that is never reached. There are several problems associated with it. Bereiter notes one; namely, that integrated activities do not ensure training basic skills such as reading.

The "integrated day," according to Lillian Weber, is the ideal toward which informal educators strive. This ideal is perfectly sound in those cases where training is not necessary. The farm boy lives an integrated day and in the process learns to ride a horse; the street child in a poor nation leads an integrated day hustling a living and in the process learns arithmetic; the immigrant child leads an integrated day and in the process learns a second language. But lacking these opportunities, other children will not learn riding, arithmetic, or a second language unless they have specific training.[47]

Another problem concerning integration is the nature of knowledge. The disciplines of knowledge can be more easily integrated at an early age. It is comparatively easy to integrate science, social studies, language skills, and economics by having children pick grapes, make grape juice, write reports, talk to another class, and go into the community and sell the grape juice for a profit. Such a project is much more difficult at the intermediate and senior high school levels. The teachers of French, chemistry, physics, and drafting do not wish their children to get together to make French bread or visit a local water reservoir. Ideally, all disciplines should be integrated, but it becomes increasingly difficult each year a child remains in school because of the complex structure of the disciplines.

Solutions to this problem may be found, but not in the foreseeable future. Ancient scholars since Aristotle have attempted to understand the nature of disciplines. Educators who suggest carelessly that all disciplines be integrated would be wise to read Schwab who differentiates among the organization, syntax, and substantive structure of disciplines.[48] In addition, learning basic skills in integrated activities simply may not be possible or, when possible, not worth the cost.

In discussing objectives, knowledge, continuity, sequence, and integration, writers have emphasized the need for efficiency. To some persons efficiency and the saving of time are bad, conjuring up the image of the assembly line, time and motion studies, and a dehumanized society. Kohl states, for example, "Time in most schools is considered a precious quantity, and teachers are upset when they feel time is wasted."[49] And so they should be. "A curriculum is simply a way of saving lost motion. It is an attempt to profit by the most obvious mistakes of the past and to make it unnecessary for the child to commit every last one of them all over again."[50]

While Kohl does not decry the wasting of time in school, I doubt that he is equally tolerant when his airline tickets are not ready on time, when his editor delays publication of one of his books, or when his secretary takes an hour to type a simple memorandum.

I am reminded of a visit with a national educational leader who toured many British primary schools shortly before they became a national obsession. He said, "The schools I visited were, on the average, far superior to American schools. It is too bad they are so inefficient." The point was simply that with a little efficiency, the British primary schools could be models of excellence and would still be able to retain the worthwhile characteristics of their programs. Humanism and efficiency with children are complementary rather than antithetical.

Aside from the curriculum problems associated with the integration of disciplines, integration may contribute to the demise of open education if carried too far.

Efforts to change the curriculum by integrating or correlating the content, or by creating new category systems into which to organize the content, are made at great risk. . . . This can be attributed partly to cognitive strain on the faculty, partly to upsetting the expectations of pupils and consequently parental distrust, and partly to faculty mores which tend to become stronger when threatened by change.[51]

If Orlosky and Smith are correct, it appears that open education is sowing its own seeds of failure in its attempt to integrate various disciplines.

Teachers

Judging by the writings of proponents, open education appears to require above average, if not superb, teachers. Brown and Precious of the Church Hill Infant and Junior School respectively, Thurmaston Leicestershire, England, point out that the integrated day is more demanding of teachers than conventional classrooms. They go on to say,

As well as being intelligent and well trained, the teacher needs to be an adjusted, resilient and sympathetic person having a fund of humour and common sense. . . . She must be sensitive to other people's feelings and attitudes as well as being aware of her own personality, her limitations and capabilities.[52]

Barth notes that for a teacher to relate individually to many children "demands an extraordinary amount of sensitivity, mobility, and energy."[53] In addition, he must "know himself," and be a "secure person." He feels obligated to point out, however, that many teachers "have turned to open education through insecurity; they are permissive because they are afraid that if they are strong the children will reject them."[54] From where then are these paragons of virtue, strength, and resourcefulness to come?

Johnson notes in Chapter 1, that "the instructional methods called for under 'open education' demand an extremely competent teacher." He goes on to say, "Any scheme that can only be carried out satisfactorily by geniuses is doomed to extremely limited application."

All teachers, however, are not geniuses. No documentation is needed; nonetheless, it is worth noting that Jackson observed teachers considered *outstanding* and found that they lacked a technical vocabulary. They rarely used such terms as defense mechanism, group cohesiveness, reinforcement schedules, and role expectations. He also found that these teachers had conceptual simplicity, that is, an avoidance of complex ideas. They indicated an uncomplicated view of causality—one cause for a given behavior. Teachers' responses were intuitive rather than rational—basing responses on impulse rather than reflection and thought. Teachers were opinionated rather than open-minded. They had narrow working definitions of common terms—one term had one meaning.[55]

Must open education teachers be sensitive, secure, and loving? Teachers have been cited for their high service orientation to clients (students),[56] but the tenderness and lovingness seemingly required of teachers in open education classrooms appear to go beyond a high service orientation. It is possible that teachers attracted to open education will possess this lovingness toward children. (To the extent Barth's findings are generalizable, this may lead to their incapacity.) The less loving teachers, many of whom are competent, may not function so well in this setting. One teacher in Los Angeles commented several years ago, "I do not love children, but they interest me. Please don't ask me to love them." This teacher was outstanding, but there is reason to believe that she would be uncomfortable in an environment that required many overt displays of affection. It is possible that a child will gain a more accurate view of life if he is exposed to different types of adults, all of whom are interested in his progress, but some of whom do not care to love him.

Leles' study in Ohio revealed numerous instances of teacher cruelty in classrooms. In a sample that included 765 elementary and secondary school teachers, he found more than two hundred items of data describing practices and situations in which educational purposes were perverted by the way teachers and other school personnel handled children. For example:

I observed a teacher mock a student (in the presence of other students) who had a speech defect.

Teachers who refuse to work with students of low ability.

They put them in a corner and practically ignore them.

Male teacher bouncing fifth-grade children against walls in the classroom.

Setting the child out in the hall with a sign around his neck so the larger children could make fun of him.

A male teacher makes children stand in a corner for day after day. Also puts a child in a closet several days at a time.[57]

Many authors have noted that teachers need to work very hard in open education classrooms. This may be because open education is synonymous with quality education. Anyone who has taught at the elementary, secondary, or college levels knows that quality teaching requires more work than average or below average teaching. The quality teacher is concerned about each child. He takes time to become knowledgeable about new instructional practices. He is constantly preparing material to individualize instruction. The list is endless.

It is regrettable if teachers in open education classrooms must work harder than those in the average traditional classroom because many teachers do not have the energy, interest, or competency to do so.

Some teachers have a high energy level, strong commitment, a live imagination, and great personal resources. However, a school system cannot be organized on the assumption that all teachers are like that. Therefore, the program offered by the school must be so tightly organized that the weaker teachers can function up to a minimum level. Where judgments are likely to be wrong, rules must be provided. Where high commitment does not exist, duties must be specified. Where personal resources are limited, routinized procedures must be established.[58]

Lack of teacher energy and inventiveness is by no means a new problem. I worked with an extremely competent teacher who was a specialist in team teaching. She was a consultant to a group of teachers trying to team teach in a school in Hawaii. On her third visit there, the teachers complained to her, "It's not working. We are exhausted. We can't go on." She replied confidently, "On the contrary, that proves it is working." It is easy to see the logic in her reply. Team teaching was causing the teachers to work harder than they ever had before, and there is good reason to believe that this increased work improved the educational program being offered children. But this conclusion raises two questions: How many teachers are willing to work that hard? How long can teachers continue at such a pace?

Even if a sufficient number of competent open education teachers could be found, there is no indication that they could sustain quality instruction for more than several months or years. Denison observed that child-centered teaching represents a sizable physical and emotional drain on the practitioner—a drain that requires frequent respite. In the end, his First Street School closed, not because it had failed to teach children, but because the staff was exhausted.[59]

Denison's observation is supported in the work of Orlosky and Smith who suggest that a change is not likely to persist if there is a constant drain on the time and energy of a faculty.[60]

It seems doubtful that there are a sufficient number of teachers who will be willing to work extremely hard for many years. Surely some persons will, but they are few. And if this is the criterion for the success of open education, it is not likely that open education will have widespread adoption. Sarason, et al., add a slightly different dimension to the problem in noting that those who are creating a community setting think and plan as though they will have adequate manpower to render the quantity and quality of services needed to the numbers of people eligible for these services. This is rarely a possibility, not only because there is not an unlimited supply of money available, but also because the supply of trained manpower is limited.[61] The same argument applies to schools. "The teaching profession is already so large that it can never comprise anything more select than a cross-section of the college-educated population."[62] The fact that open education seems to require such a competent work force is a major obstacle to its widespread adoption.

Parent, Governance, Socioeconomic Class

Parent involvement in schools has increased with the emergence of open education although factors other than open education have been principally responsible for this increased involvement. The problems associated with increased citizen involvement are largely political and social in nature. The following types of questions arise: (1) What are the rights of parents to educate their own children? (2) Who is going to govern schools? (3) What are the attitudes of parents and children from lower socioeconomic levels?

Rights of Parents

The argument that parents should have the right to determine the type of education offered their children is stated by Bereiter in the *Harvard Educational Review*. He asserts that "parents typically educate, and it is my contention . . . that they are the only ones who have a clear-cut right to educate."[63] This point of view would have merit if all parents were interested in the education of their children. Unfortunately, however, some parents are not, and those who are not may have children most in need of education. Furthermore, the educational program espoused by a parent in the mountains of West Virginia, the plains of North Dakota, or the ghettos of Los Angeles may not prepare a child for citizenship, an aim that Bereiter deems important. There are a distressingly high number of parents who believe every murderer should be shot, blacks are inferior, prisons too lenient, a woman's place is in the home, and that America should drop a hydrogen bomb on China.

The voucher plan, as proposed by Jencks and others, would permit parents to enroll their children in a school of their choice. This plan runs the danger of undermining a democratic state as it permits parents who are often bigoted concerning race and religion, and provincial concerning economic and political philosophy to send their children to schools with persons of similar biases. Katz asks, "What kind of educational change can be accomplished by exchanging one arbitrary educational authority for another?"[64]

Hutchins challenges Jencks' and Bereiter's arguments:

Every child must be given the chance to become the kind of citizen the First Amendment demands. This obligation is too important to be left to parents. The community compels them to allow their children to have this opportunity either by offering the education itself or through institutions it approves.[65]

In addition, Hutchins points out that the community includes bachelors, spinsters, childless couples, and the elderly—all of whom are interested in the benefits from its schools.

The aims of society transcend the aims of parents just as they transcend the aims of individual students. Indeed, a major intent of schooling is to seek to erase the hideous scars that have been made by parents who have intentionally or inadvertently indoctrinated their children into believing their often erroneous biases concerning man and his responsibility toward his fellow man. Such a position is not intended to convey that all or even a majority of parents are bigoted and ignorant, but it challenges the opposite assumption that all or a majority of parents are interested and qualified to provide for their children's education.

Governance of Schools

Citizens seek to enlarge their control of schools. This movement comes at the same time that teachers seek to increase their autonomy from lay control. Klein, an advocate of community participation, reviews the traditional argument against citizen participation: lack of expertise, insufficient time, too personal and biased perspective, and lack of technical competence. He notes also that professional decision making is quicker, more rational, scientifically based, and less distorted by local biases and individual prejudice. He argues, however, that professional decision making contributes to the weakening of the community since it tends to promote insecurity by taking the control of events outside the citizens' sphere of influence.[66]

Citizen involvement may have desirable effects on the educational program; but in which areas are they to be involved—instruction, staff selection, curriculum? While instruction is not a science, few parents know how to teach modern mathematics, how to generate enthusiasm and intellectual curiosity in students, which activities to include in science, how to assist children write a short verse, etc. Similarly, I question whether laymen can do a better job selecting teachers than teachers themselves. So far as curriculum is concerned, a case can be made for teachers listening too closely to the demands of parents.

It is clear that there is a decided power struggle between teachers and citizens. No teacher wishes to establish an educational program autonomous of lay control. Teachers do not wish to advance their well-being over the diminution of the well-being of citizens. Citizens should ponder whether their involvement will come at the expense of the professional development of teachers[67] and, thus, possibly at the expense of the educational program being offered students.

Lower Socioeconomic Class
Resistance

Open education may be unsuccessful with lower socioeconomic class children, especially blacks and Puerto Ricans. Levy spent a year studying children, teachers, and parents in an all black and Puerto Rican elementary school located in a ghetto. He noted that most of the teachers were concerned primarily with controlling rather than educating children. At the beginning of the school year, twenty-five members of the staff were classified as "acute." This represented about one half of the staff.

An acute teacher is likely to attempt a soft line with the children. He may greet his class informally, not demand that they keep a perfectly straight line to the classroom and not try immediately to establish rigid routines. . . . The children do not take up the bargain on his terms. . . . If he fails to clamp down on talking, eating, and moving around, the children talk, eat, move, and leave the classroom as much as possible.[68]

The acute teacher naively believes the children will be sensitive to *his* problems. When they are not, he becomes angry. He begins to shout, demands quiet, requires them to remain in their seats and to refrain from eating. Unfortunately, however, these demands are ineffective. Gradually, the teacher threatens to send children to the principal's office, writes notes to parents, or has them suspended by the administration.

But the shouting and threatening fail to pacify the children. . . . The more the teacher screams at the children, pounds his fist on the table, and chases them around the room, the greater their delight in the victory. . . . The children's energy and staying power are limitless.[69]

Twenty-one of twenty-five acute teachers became chronic or control teachers by the end of the year.

Levy's experience was nearly identical to the open education teachers described by Barth. "The children's abuse of teachers, materials, and themselves presented an overriding priority: to get the children under control."[70]

Levy concludes that the ghetto school's task is the exact opposite of its stated purpose. It prepares children for life in the ghetto. "If Midway's task is to change, the change will probably not result from events that occur within the school but from larger battles, broader realignments, more pervasive changes in American society."[71] Featherstone notes, "I would guess, the macro issue of race is so important that to promote open classrooms without dealing with the racial climate of the schools is futile."[72] Kozol too makes a similar point concerning the irrelevance of freer types of education.

"Wow!" I hear some of these free-school people say, "We made an Iroquois canoe out of a log!" Nobody, however, *needs* an Iroquois canoe. Even the Iroquois do not. The Iroquois can buy aluminum canoes if they should really need them. They don't however. What they need are doctors, lawyers, teachers, organizers, labor leaders. . . . There may be some pedagogic value or therapeutic function in this form of simulation for the heartsick or disoriented son or grandson of a rich man. It does not, however, correspond to my idea of struggle and survival in the streets and cities I know.[73] (Italics in the original)

The point is simply that "America's communication with its lower classes takes place within a political context which transcends the intentions of its welfare liberals."[74] Open education is unrealistic in the setting in which ghetto children live.

My observations in visiting open education classrooms in New York parallel the views of Levy and Kozol. In one "Open Corridor" school in New York City, black parents did not take full advantage of the opportunity to enroll their children in the experimental program. In an urban center in upstate New York, middle and upper-middle class white parents proudly volunteered to bus their children across town into a low socioeconomic level neighborhood. When the open education program did not stress training in basic skills, the white parents were surprised when black parents withdrew their children and enrolled them in a traditional school.

Another factor is the noninstrumentalism of most open education classrooms. In the traditional view, Head Start (apparent in its title) is seen as preparatory for kindergarten; kindergarten children are taught to sit in rows to prepare them for first grade; the elementary school is intended to prepare children for intermediate school, and so on up the line.

While instrumentalism is being criticized by white educators, black parents are beginning to endorse it as a way of improving their children's future. " 'We want our children to go to high school, to college, to get a good, white-collar job, to have a home, a car, and raise a family. In short, we want them to do what *you* (whites) have done.' "[75] (Italics in the original)

Black parents increasingly give less consideration to what is enjoyable today and think in terms of preparing for a brighter future for their children tomorrow. If open education rejects traditional methods of coercive student control, requires cooperative students, attaches minimum emphasis on the three Rs, and is noninstrumental, it will likely be either superfluous or harmful to children in the ghetto. Parents from lower socioeconomic levels will almost certainly resist it.

Conclusion[76]

1. As of this writing, it appears that open education will not soon be defined as a discrete concept and will remain a multidimensional ideology. Many of the dimensions associated with open education can be found in the better English primary schools. It is a healthy tendency to seek out such tried-and-true methods and combine them for optimum effectiveness, but it is a mistake to see this "package" as substantially different from good education.

2. Open education is not an alternative to traditional education; it is an attempt to improve traditional education. "Good" open education classrooms are synonymous with "good" traditional classrooms.

3. Open education will not be adopted widely in the United States. It would be unwise to believe, for example, that open education would have much more of a widespread adoption in the seventies than the nongraded school had in the sixties, since the "concepts" are comparable in many ways. The following items represent the reasons for this skepticism:

a. Open education is a nascent ideology. Emerging ideologies are difficult to implement because they cannot be defined operationally. It has been shown that concrete innovations, such as overhead projectors, are far easier to institute than such ideologies as progressive education.

b. There are not nearly enough competent, loving, secure, and hardworking teachers to implement open education on a wide scale. This is not meant to suggest that all teachers are incompetent, unloving, insecure, or lazy. The view would apply to virtually any occupational group. It is intended only to reinforce the view that open education is too dependent upon the exceptional teacher to enjoy widespread adoption.

c. Administrative support which is normally imperative will depend largely on the desires of the citizenry. Parents are not likely to accept an educational program that is not instrumental.

d. Evangelistic teachers are drawn to open education and will be inclined to change substantially many dimensions of open education. In so doing, they will lay the groundwork for their own failure. Since open education is multidimensional, its cognitive load on teachers is heavy and, thus will not enjoy permanent change. The high hopes and enthusiasm will decrease as the weight of tradition overcomes them.

e. Many proponents of open education are anti-curriculum, continuity, sequence, knowledge, and a few are preposterously anti-instruction. Such a naive position will often lead to chaos and misapplication.

4. Where open education is adopted, it will usually be in name only, with little significant change in the educational program. We can expect a limited surge of so-called open education classrooms like the so-called nongraded schools of the sixties.

5. Where open education is adopted, it will usually be at the lower grades.

6. There will be a strong resistance to the adoption of open education at the intermediate and senior high school levels because most parents and teachers view education as instrumental, and integration is more difficult to achieve at these levels.

7. Open education will be relatively ineffective with lower socioeconomic class children for a variety of reasons. (a) It is doubtful that any type of educational program will be sufficiently powerful to offset the multiplicity of social and political factors that affect the lives of children in the ghetto. (b) Such children are less compliant. (c) Open education does not ensure or even emphasize the necessity of mastery of basic skills. Regardless of the so-called humaneness of open education, the most humane program for lower socioeconomic class children may be a strong program of training in the basic skills by programed or computer instruction.

8. Parents of lower socioeconomic level children will likely reject open education because it is noninstrumental, does not emphasize the mastery of basic skills, is too permissive, and does not demonstrate its superiority over traditional programs.

9. Parents will increasingly be given the option of enrolling their children in an open education classroom. This increase of parental autonomy will likely collide head on with the growing militancy of teacher associations as they strive for increased autonomy.

10. Released time or extensive in-service training for teachers and administrators is imperative if open education is to be practiced successfully on a wide scale. "If teachers must be retrained in order for a change to be made, as in team teaching, the chances for success are reduced unless strong incentives to be retrained are provided."[77] Extensive in-service training seems unlikely.

Duke voices caution in interpreting conclusions concerning emerging ideologies since they can become self-fulfilling prophecies. "Schoolmen read a critical set of predictive conclusions and then proceed to lose interest or oppose what may have the potential of being a worthwhile innovation."[78] The critical conclusions are not based on the belief that open education lacks vitality and promise, but that other factors such as the lack of qualified teachers and community resistance to new programs may result in a stillborn ideology, one which deserves more of an opportunity to develop. Lady Bridget Plowden has emphasized how slow the rate of improvement has been in England despite extra funding for teachers, materials, and buildings.

I strongly believe that schoolmen, and particularly educational researchers, are obligated to examine open education critically for needed modification or outright rejection. To do otherwise would be a disservice both to the research community in education and to the children in schools. To paraphrase Kozol, there is a time when we must sit down and compose rhapsodic stories about open education; there is another time when we have to be as honest as we can. Now is the time for candor.

Notes

Notes

Introduction

1. Joseph Featherstone, "Schools for Children: What's Happening in British Classrooms," *The New Republic* (August 19, 1967), 17-21.

2. Joseph Featherstone, "How Children Learn," *The New Republic* (September 2, 1967), 17-21.

3. Joseph Featherstone, "Teaching Children to Think," *The New Republic* (September 9, 1967), 15-19.

4. Bassett's analysis of educational innovations in America and Great Britain can be found in G.W. Bassett, *Innovation in Primary Education* (London: Wiley-Interscience, 1970).

5. Articles concerning the British Primary School had appeared before those of Featherstone's. They were few in number, however, and did not have nearly so widespread an impact.

6. It should be noted that the term "open education" is not used in England. When the British use such a term, it is most often the "integrated day."

Chapter 1
A Skeptic's View

1. Donald A. Myers and Daniel L. Duke, "Elementary School Appraisal—The Status of Open Education in New York State Elementary Schools, 1971-1972," unpublished manuscript, p. 57.

2. Charles E. Silberman, *Crisis in the Classroom: The Remaking of American Education* (New York: Random House, 1970).

3. "Open Education," The University of the State of New York, The State Education Department, Division of Education for the Disadvantaged, n.d.

4. Herbert J. Walberg and Susan Christie Thomas, "Open Education: An Operational Definition and Validation in Great Britain and United States," *American Educational Research Journal*, IX (Spring, 1972), 206.

5. G.W.J. Crawford, "The Primary School: A Balanced View," *The Crisis in Education*, Black Paper Two, ed. C.B. Cox and A.E. Dyson (London: Critical Quarterly Society, 1969), p. 96.

6. Lionel Elvin, "The Positive Roles of Society and the Teacher," *Perspectives on Plowden*, ed. R.S. Peters (London: Routledge & Kegan Paul, 1969), pp. 102-103. [U.S. publishers, Humanities Press, Inc.]

7. Robert Dearden, "The Aims of Primary Education," *Perspectives on Plowden*, ibid., p. 24.

8. Crawford, op. cit., p. 98.

9. James D. Koerner, "The Greening of the Schools," *Reactions to Silberman's Crisis in the Classroom*, ed. A. Harry Passow (Worthington, Ohio: Charles A. Jones, 1971), p. 13.

10. Ibid., p. 16.

11. R.S. Peters (ed.), "A Recognizable Philosophy of Education: A Constructive Critique," *Perspectives on Plowden*, op. cit., p. 12.

12. Dearden, op. cit., p. 33.

13. C.B. Cox and A.E. Dyson (eds.), *The Black Papers on Education* (London: Davis-Poynter, Ltd., 1971), p. 17.

14. Dearden, op. cit., p. 29.

15. Kenneth Simpson, "Music in Schools: The Problem of Teaching," *Goodbye Mr. Short*, Black Paper Three, ed. C.B. Cox and A.E. Dyson (London: Critical Quarterly Society, 1970), p. 82.

16. D.M. Pinn, "What Kind of Primary School?" *The Crisis in Education*, op. cit., p. 102.

17. Dearden, op. cit., p. 35.

18. A.E. Dyson, "The Sleep of Reason," *The Black Papers on Education*, op. cit., pp. 85, 86.

19. Stuart Froome, *Why Tommy Isn't Learning* (London: Tom Stacey, Ltd., 1970), p. 153.

20. Crawford, op. cit., p. 99.

21. Peters, op. cit., p. 12.

Chapter 2
Origins and Antecedents

1. From *Crisis in the Classroom*, by Charles E. Silberman. Copyright © by Charles E. Silberman. (New York: Vintage Books, A Division of Random House, 1970), pp. 179-80. Reprinted by permission of Random House, Inc.

2. These include John and Evelyn Dewey's *Schools of Tomorrow*, Mayhew and Edwards' *Dewey School*, Graham's *Progressive Education: From Arcady to Academe*, ASCD's *A New Look at Progressive Education*, Caroline Pratt's *I Learn from Children*, Lucy Sprague Mitchell's *The Little Red School House*, Washburne's *New School in the Old World*, Rugg and Shumaker's *The Child Centered School*, and Neill's *Summerhill*.

3. The most definitive history and analysis of the child-centered school can be found in Lawrence A. Cremin's *Transformation of the School* (New York: Random House, 1964).

4. John Amos Comenius, "The Great Didactic," as quoted in Silberman, op. cit., p. 113.

5. Seventh Annual Report, in Lawrence A. Cremin (ed.), *The Republic and the School: Horace Mann on the Education of Free Men* (New York: Teachers College Press, 1957).

6. Frederick Burk, as quoted in Silberman, op. cit., p. 167.

7. Dewey's school, like so many other efforts led by those with an idea, transformed substantially after Dewey's departure from the University of Chicago. Its growth and change illustrate what happens when an effort or a movement is the shadow cast by one man. Similar fates befell developments by Marietta Johnson and J.L. Merriam and later by persons like James Chritzberg and James Tipton.

8. John Dewey, *The Child and the Curriculum* (Chicago: The University of Chicago Press, 1902).

9. Benjamin S. Bloom, *Stability and Change in Human Characteristics* (New York: John Wiley & Sons, Inc. 1964).

10. C.H. Dobinson, *Jean-Jacques Rousseau* (London: Methuen & Co., Ltd., 1969), pp. 77 ff.

11. From the book *Schools of Tomorrow* by John and Evelyn Dewey. Copyright 1915 by E.P. Dutton & Co., Inc. Renewal, 1943 by John and Evelyn Dewey. Paperback edition copyright © 1962 by E.P. Dutton & Co., Inc., publishers, and used with their permission.

12. *Children and Their Primary Schools*, Vol. I (London: Her Majesty's Stationery Office, 1967), paragraph 523.

13. Dewey and Dewey, op. cit., p. 76.

14. Ibid., pp. 78-79.

15. Jerome Bruner, *The Process of Education* (Cambridge, Mass.: Harvard University Press, 1962).

16. Consultative Committee of the Board of Education, *The Primary School* (London: His Majesty's Stationery Office, 1931).

17. See D.E.M. Gardner, *Experiment and Tradition in the Primary School* (London: Methuen & Co., Ltd., 1966); *Education of Young Children* (London: Methuen & Co., Ltd., 1956); *Education Under Sight* (London: Methuen & Co., Ltd., 1949); *The Children's Play Center* (London: Methuen & Co., Ltd., 1939).

18. See Susan Isaacs, *The Children We Teach* (London: University of London Press, 1963) [New York: Schocken Books, Inc., © 1971]; *The Educational Value of the Nursery School* (London: Nursery School Association of Great Britain and Northern Ireland, No. 45); *Childhood and After* (London: Routledge & Kegan Paul, Ltd., 1948) [New York: Agathon Press, Inc., 1970]; *Social Development in Young Children* (London: Routledge and Kegan Paul, Ltd., 1933); *Intellectual Growth in Young Children* (London: Routledge and Kegan Paul, Ltd., 1930) [New York: Schocken Books, Inc., 1966]. See also Nathan Isaacs, *The Growth of Understanding in the Young Child* (London: Ward Lock Educational, 1961) [New York: Agathon Press, Inc., 1971]; *New Light on Children's Ideas of Number* (London: Ward Lock Educational, 1960) [New York: Agathon Press, Inc., 1971]; *Early Scientific Trends in Children* (London: National Froebel Foundation, 1958).

19. Ruth Griffiths, *Imagination and Early Childhood* (London: Routledge & Kegan Paul, Ltd., 1945).

20. During the winter term, I asked one hundred "randomly" met English infant school teachers if (1) they had read the Plowden Report, and (2) if they had found it challenging and useful. Less than fifty percent reported they had read it. The largest portion by far of those who had read it, said they long since felt they had accepted and sought to practice the major ideas presented.

21. The British school teacher's definition of "stretching" is elusive, but the idea is very well understood and important. It expresses the teacher's intention of helping a child to "try his hand or his mind" on a new or more difficult undertaking without consideration for ever threatening comparison with others or with some teacher standard so general in the United States.

22. Much is made by some Americans of the impact of official documents in Britain. They point to the Hadow Report, the Robbins Report, the Newson Report as pronouncements with great effect. One would have to agree that some parts of some reports, like the James Report, affect legislation and subsequent practice, but it must be pointed out that government reports tend in Britain to confirm what has already been widely agreed to or emerged in practice. Plowden didn't create the sentiments among British educators. The ideas and the practices were already there. They are presented and discussed in "Nursery and Infant Schools," Chapter II, in W.A.L. Blyth's authoritative two-volume work, *English Primary Education*, published by Routledge and Kegan Paul, London, 1965, timed to precede the issuance of *Children and Their Primary Schools* and to provide a "comprehensive work which combines a general sociological description of English primary education with a survey of the results of sociological investigations."

23. Outstanding among these were Colonel Parker's School at the end of the last century, Dewey's school at the University of Chicago; Caroline Pratt's City and County School; Marietta Johnson's Fairhope; Alabama organic plan, the Lincoln School; and J.H. Merriam's four-factor effort at the University Elementary School at Columbia, Missouri, and Washburne's Winnetka reform by contrast were public school efforts, supported then by a far less prestigious body than the Plowden Committee. There were indeed other adventurers, notably in Denver, in Menomonie, Wisconsin, and Greenwich, Connecticut. But records about them are sparse, and they have somehow unfortunately been lumped into a category of copyists, adaptors, and aborters who ran amok, so misinterpreting Dewey's principles that the philosopher repudiated them in his famous rebuke in *The New Republic* and subsequently in *Experience and Education*.

24. Ellsworth Collings, *An Experiment with a Project Curriculum* (New York: The Macmillan Company, 1923).

25. William Heard Kilpatrick, *Project Method: The Use of the Purposeful Act in the Educative Process* (New York: Teachers College, Columbia University, 1918).

26. C.B. Cox and A.E. Dyson (eds.), "Fight for Education," *The Critical Quarterly Society*, London, 1969.

27. Responsible British educators are exasperated by some of their own countrymen who offer inaccurate descriptions of English practice to avid American ears. American commercial institutions and foundations have produced rosy propaganda films which suggest environments far more enriched and enlivened than exist in but a limited number of British schools.

28. K.B. Start and B.K. Wells, "The Trend of Reading Standards," National Foundation for Educational Research, Slough, 1972.

29. Henry Brickell, *Organizing New York State for Educational Change* (Albany: New York State Education Department, 1960).

30. Silberman, op. cit., p. 319.

31. Ibid., p. 321.

Chapter 3
Stages in Implementation

1. Three books by Dewey are especially relevant. In 1915, he and Evelyn Dewey published perhaps the most practical book for the classroom teacher, even to this day. It was entitled, *Schools of Tomorrow* (New York: E.P. Dutton & Co., Inc., 1915). The following year he published a book that explicated his basic philosophy of education. It was entitled, *Democracy in Education: An Introduction to the Philosophy of Education* (New York: The Macmillan Company, 1916). A third reference that is of practical use to teachers is *Experience and Education* (New York: The Macmillan Company, 1938). This book was written principally to clarify progressive education to those disciples who were falsely interpreting it.

2. Jean Piaget and Bärbel Inhelder, *The Psychology of the Child* (New York: Basic Books, Inc., 1969).

3. Two documents that support these suggested stages are Anne M. Bussis and Edward A. Chittenden, "Teacher Perspective on Change to an Open Approach," Paper presented at the Annual American Educational Research Association Conference, New York, March, 1972. Also, "Open Corridor Teacher's Diagnostic Instrument," Mimeographed document from City College of New York Advisory Service, 1972.

4. E.S.E.A. Title I, "Open Education: Theresa, Theater and Terrariums" (Albany, New York: The State Education Department, 1971).

5. James B. MacDonald and Esther Zarat, "Study of Openness in Classroom Interactions" (Milwaukee, Wisconsin: University of Milwaukee, 1966), mimeographed.

6. For a detailed and scholarly analysis of the gradualist approach, see Amitai Etzioni, *Studies in Social Change* (New York: Holt, Rinehart & Winston, 1966), pp. 64-78.

Chapter 4
The Opening of an Open School

1. Marilyn Hapgood, "The Open Classroom: Protect It From Its Friends," *Saturday Review* (September 18, 1971), 66.

2. Vivian S. Sherman, *Two Contrasting Educational Models: Applications and Policy Implications* (Menlo Park, Calif.: Stanford Research Institute, 1970).

3. Mauritz Johnson, Jr., "Definitions and Models in Curriculum Theory," *Educational Theory*, XVII, No. 2 (April, 1967).

4. In developing this study, I was influenced by the insightful case study of the Kensington Elementary School reported by Louis M. Smith and Pat M. Keith in *Anatomy of Educational Innovation*. Their methodology and treatment of data were extremely useful to me. In addition, after reading Barth's *Open Education and the American School*, I was pleased and at the same time displeased that his findings so closely paralleled mine. "In September, desks were in clusters, diverse instructional materials were in abundance, teachers were kind and unobtrusive, and the children were offered considerable freedom. By December, desks were in rows, textbooks were in use, teachers yelled and were in front of the room, and the children divided into groups by ability with little freedom of movement." Pp. 111-12.

5. Louis M. Smith and Pat M. Keith, *Anatomy of Educational Innovation: An Organizational Analysis of an Elementary School* (New York: John Wiley & Sons, Inc., 1971), pp. 21-35.

6. Vincent R. Rogers, *The English Primary School* (New York: The Macmillan Company, 1970); Mary Brown and Norman Precious, *The Integrated Day in the Primary School* (London: Ward Lock Educational Co., Ltd., 1968) (New York: Agathon Press, Inc., 1970); Roland S. Barth and Charles H. Rathbone, *A Bibliography of Open Education* (Newton, Mass.: Early Childhood Education Study, 1971); Lady Bridget Plowden, Chairman, *Children and their Primary Schools: A Report of the Central Advisory Council for Education* (London: Her Majesty's Stationery Office, 1966).

7. Roland S. Barth, *Open Education and the American School* (New York: Agathon Press, Inc., 1972), p. 118. © 1972 by Roland S. Barth.

8. Smith and Keith, op. cit., p. 101.

9. State Education Department, "Information and Planning Kit on Open Education," Albany, New York, 1970.

10. Hilda Taba, *Curriculum Development: Theory and Practice* (New York: Harcourt, Brace & World, 1962); Mauritz Johnson, op. cit.; B.O. Smith, W.O. Stanley, and J. Harlan Shores, *Fundamentals of Curriculum Development* (New York: Harcourt, Brace & World, 1950); John I. Goodlad and Maurice N. Richter, *The Development of a Conceptual System for Dealing with Problems of Curriculum and Instruction* (Los Angeles: Institute for the Development of Educational Activities, 1966); et al.

11. Smith and Keith, op. cit., p. 85.

12. Ibid., pp. 22, 49, 53.

13. Donald Orlosky and B. Othanel Smith, "Educational Change: Its Origins and Characteristics," *Phi Delta Kappan*, LIII (March, 1972), 414.

14. Barth, op. cit., p. 171.

15. Smith and Keith, op. cit., pp. 79-88.

16. Barth, op. cit., p. 142.

17. Ibid., p. 174.

18. Smith and Keith, op. cit., p. 83.

19. Ibid.

20. Seymour B. Sarason, George Zitnay, and Frances Kaplan Grossman, *The Creation of a Community Setting* (Syracuse, New York: Syracuse University Division of Special Education and Rehabilitation and the Center on Human Policy, 1971), p. 42.

21. Barth, op. cit., p. 210.

22. Smith and Keith, op. cit., p. 53.

Chapter 5
Status in New York State

1. Persons may question the generalizability of our findings. In this regard, it should be noted that while New York State differs substantially from many states, the investigators view it as a prototype for those states in which open education is being supported by the state department of education and several universities. The findings may not be applicable where there is a lack of support from these organizations. It should be noted that New York State is largely rural except for the New York City standard metropolitan area, Buffalo, Rochester, and the Albany area.

2. While there is no definitive definition, Walberg and Thomas have been at work to define open education. See Herbert J. Walberg and Susan Christie Thomas, "Open Education: An Operational Definition and Validation in Great Britain and United States," *American Educational Research Journal*, IX (Spring 1972), 197-208.

3. John Blackie, *Inside the Primary School* (London: HMSO, 1967, in U.S. British Information Services, New York, New York 10022); Mary Brown and Norman Precious, *The Integrated Day in the Primary School* (New York: Agathon Press, Inc., 1968). Joseph Featherstone, *Schools Where Children Learn* (New York: Liveright, 1971); Charles H. Rathbone (ed.), *Open Education: The Informal Classroom* (New York: Citation Press, 1971); Vincent R. Rogers (ed.), *Teaching in the British Primary School* (New York: The Macmillan Company, 1970); Lillian Weber, *The English Infant School and Informal Education* (Englewood Cliffs, New Jersey: Prentice-Hall, Inc., 1971).

4. A.S. Neill, *Summerhill: A Radical Approach to Child Rearing* (New York: Hart Publishing Company, 1960); Paul Goodman, *Compulsory Mis-Education* (New York: Horizon Press, 1964); Ivan Illich, *Deschooling Society* (New York: Harrow Books, Harper & Row, Publishers, 1970); Jonathon Kozol, "The Open Schoolroom: New Words for Old Deceptions," *Ramparts*, XI (July, 1972), 38-41.

5. Some free schools are "free" in name only and one strains to find any differences between them and open education classrooms or even traditional classrooms. Both Marin and Kozol make note of this fact.

6. Delimitations are as follows:

(1) No concrete definitions of open education exist, thus, it is hazardous to make generalizations about the findings.

(2) Since there is no comprehensive or definitive list of schools engaged in open education, no claim is made to having selected a random sample. Generalizations drawn from the data should be viewed as tentative and suggestive. It should be noted, however, that the sample included a wide range of types of communities, student enrollment, and socioeconomic levels.

(3) Approximately three hours were spent in each school. Additional time in schools might have altered the findings.

(4) The principal, and normally the teachers, knew investigators were going to visit. It is possible that they "put on a show" for the visitors.

(5) Only two schools were selected in New York City, yet it may contain as many open education classrooms as exist in the remainder of the state. Additional schools from this area might have altered the findings, particularly the means for type of community and socioeconomic levels. In addition, the schools visited in New York City were part of Lillian Weber's network of "Open Corridor" schools. Because of their comparatively long experience (five years) in open education and their association with Lillian Weber and her staff, it seems possible that these school programs would be more advanced than others in the city. This assumption may be offset by the fact that the schools with which she works are considered "difficult" schools.

(6) No reliability coefficient was obtained for a third investigator who visited two schools.

7. Charles E. Silberman, *Crisis in the Classroom: The Remaking of American Education* (New York: Random House, 1970).

8. John I. Goodlad and M. Frances Klein, and Associates, *Behind the Classroom Door* (Worthington, Ohio: Charles A. Jones Publishing Company, 1970).

9. Kozol, op. cit., pp. 38-41.

Chapter 6
Alternative Schools

1. This estimate is derived from Allen Graubard, "The Free School Movement," *Harvard Educational Review*, XLII (August, 1972), 356-58. The

350-400 schools mentioned by Graubard are estimated to enroll from 11,500 to 13,000 students of various ages. It should be observed, however, that these approximations are based on nonpublic schools only. In addition, only schools that were functioning were counted. By 1972 many alternatives had ceased operations. I would guess that more than 1,000 public and nonpublic alternatives have come into existence since 1965.

2. For a further discussion of this notion of the universality of good teaching, see Donald A. Myers and Daniel L. Duke, *Elementary School Appraisal—The Status of Open Education in New York State Elementary Schools, 1971-72* (an unpublished study).

3. One major boost to the idea of alternative schools was the federal Experimental Schools Program. In both 1971 and 1972, large grants were made to three districts for the development of multiple alternatives "within the system."

4. I am currently completing a tour of more than 50 public and nonpublic alternative schools east of the Mississippi River. In very few instances have I encountered marked differences in instructional methodology, evaluation techniques, or curricular organization. It would appear that there simply are not an unlimited number of ways to teach, evaluate, or structure intended learnings.

5. For a detailed analysis of decision making see Daniel Linden Duke, "Decision-Making in the Alternative School" (unpublished manuscript).

6. Reprinted by permission of the publisher from Sloan R. Wayland, "The Teacher as Decision-Maker," in A. Harry Passow, editor, *Curriculum Crossroads*, (New York: Teachers College Press, copyright 1962 by Teachers College, Columbia University), p. 43.

7. James Anderson, "The Authority Structure of the School: System of Social Exchange," *Educational Administration Quarterly*, III (Spring, 1967), 144-45.

8. My appreciation is extended to John Sakala, Director of the Home Base School in Watertown, Massachusetts, for this observation.

9. For a detailed discussion of professionalism versus bureaucratization, see Charles E. Bidwell, "The School as a Formal Organization," *Handbook of Organizations*, ed. James G. March (Chicago: Rand McNally, 1965), pp. 972-1022.

10. Jacob W. Getzels, "Administration as a Social Process," *Administrative Theory in Education*, ed. Andrew W. Halpin (Chicago: Midwest Administration Center, 1958), p. 161.

11. For a full discussion of formal and informal organization, consult Daniel E. Griffiths, "Administration as Decision Making," *Administrative Theory in Education*, ibid., pp. 126-29.

12. I am indebted to Judy Adrezin of the State University of New York at Albany, Department of Curriculum and Instruction for helping in the development of the concepts of formal and informal decision making.

13. Robert C. Riordan, *Alternative Schools in Action* (Bloomington, Indiana: Phi Delta Kappa Educational Foundation, 1972), p. 10.

14. My appreciation to Professor Arnold Foster of the State University of New York at Albany, Department of Sociology, for elaborating on this theme.

15. Michael B. Katz, *Class, Bureaucracy and Schools* (New York: Praeger Publishers, Inc., 1971), p. 122.

16. Paul R. Mort, "Studies in Educational Innovation from the Institute of Administrative Research: An Overview," *Innovation in Education*, ed. Matthew B. Miles (New York: Teachers College Press, 1967), pp. 317-28.

17. Anton C. Zijderveld, *The Abstract Society: A Cultural Analysis of Our Time* (Garden City, New York: Anchor Books, 1971), p. 10. © 1971 by Doubleday and Company.

18. Amitai Etzioni, *Modern Organizations* (Englewood Cliffs, New Jersey: Prentice-Hall, Inc., 1964), p. 10.

19. For a concise treatment of the dimensions of bureaucratic organization, see Peter M. Blau, "Weber's Theory of Bureaucracy," *Max Weber*, ed. Dennis Wrong (Englewood Cliffs, New Jersey: Prentice-Hall, Inc., 1970), pp. 141-45.

20. John Patenade and Marge Hart, "Demythicizing Movements," *The New Schools Exchange Newsletter*, No. 85 (October 31, 1972), 2-3.

21. Peter Schrag, "End of the Impossible Dream," *Saturday Review* (September 19, 1970), 68-70.

22. Allen Graubard, "The Free School Movement," *Harvard Educational Review*, XLII (August, 1972), 366.

23. Ibid., p. 365.

24. Ibid., pp. 365-66.

25. Ibid., pp. 366-67.

26. Ibid., pp. 367-68.

27. The assumptions on which this alternative typology are based are derived from the author's field investigations and will be included in a forthcoming work entitled *From Custodian to Community: The Challenge of the Radical Alternative School.*

28. Unfortunately for the radical ideals of many alternative school families, mothers often wind up being the most involved members. An argument can be made that the middle class, parent-operated alternative school is a women's organization, since women generally have more flexible schedules.

29. My appreciation to Mark I. Berger of the State University of New York at Albany, Department of Educational Foundations, for suggesting this idea.

30. Jonathan Kozol, "Moving on—to Nowhere," *Saturday Review* (December 9, 1972), p. 6.

31. Carl Bereiter, "Schools without Education," *Harvard Educational Review*, XLII (August, 1972), 390-413.

32. Lawrence A. Cremin, *The Transformation of the School* (New York: Random House, 1964).

33. Paul N. Ylvisaker, "Beyond '72: Strategies for Schools," *Saturday Review* (November 11, 1972), 33.

34. Amitai Etzioni, "Human Beings Are Not Very Easy to Change After All," *Saturday Review* (June 3, 1972), 47.

35. See the discussion of technocratic societies in Theodore Roszak, *The Making of a Counter Culture: Reflections on the Technocratic Society and its Youthful Opposition* (Garden City, New York: Doubleday & Company, Inc., 1969).

36. For a thorough discussion of temporary organizations, see Warren Bennis and Philip Slater, *The Temporary Society* (New York: Harper & Row, Publishers, 1968), and Alvin Toffler, *Future Shock* (New York: Bantam Books, Inc., 1971), pp. 124-51.

Chapter 7
Critical Issues

1. Peter Marin, "The Free School Nonmovement: Has Imagination Outstripped Reality?" *Saturday Review*, LV (July 22, 1972), 42.

2. Vivian S. Sherman, *Two Contrasting Educational Models: Applications and Policy Implications* (Menlo Park, Calif.: Stanford Research Institute, 1970), p. 11.

3. Ibid., p. 25.

4. My appreciation to Daniel Duke for his assistance in the above analysis.

5. Anne M. Bussis and Edward A. Chittenden, *Analysis of an Approach to Open Education* (Princeton, New Jersey: Educational Testing Service, 1970). The other two investigators were Marianne Amarel and Masako N. Tanaka.

6. Ibid., pp. 24-25.

7. Ibid., p. 24.

8. Ibid., p. 22.

9. Ibid., p. 26.

10. Roland S. Barth, "Open Education: Assumptions about Learning and Knowledge," unpublished doctoral dissertation, Harvard University, 1970.

11. Charles H. Rathbone, "Open Education and the Teacher," unpublished doctoral dissertation, Harvard University, 1970.

12. Herbert J. Walberg and Susan Christie Thomas, "Open Education: An Operational Definition and Validation in Great Britain and United States," *American Educational Research Journal*, IX (Spring, 1972), 200-201. © by American Educational Research Association, Washington, D.C.

13. Ibid., p. 206.

14. Specifically, they state: "At grades 1-3 significance [.05 or .10] was achieved in the (1) flexible use of space, (2) warmth and acceptance of the teacher, (3) teacher responding and reacting, (4) pupil soliciting and reacting and (5) total teacher moves and total pupil moves." Bruce W. Tuchman, David W. Cochran, and Eugene J. Travers, "Evaluating the Open Classroom," paper

presented at the American Educational Research Association, February, 1°73, p. 8.

15. Ibid.

16. Walberg and Thomas, op. cit., p. 198.

17. Ibid., p. 202.

18. Seymour B. Sarason, George Zitnay, and Frances Kaplan Grossman, *The Creation of a Community Setting* (Syracuse, New York: Syracuse University Division of Special Education and Rehabilitation and the Center on Human Policy, 1971), p. 71.

19. Walberg and Thomas, op. cit., p. 198.

20. Roland S. Barth, *Open Education and the American School* (New York: Agathon Press, Inc., 1972), p. 212. © 1972 by Roland S. Barth.

21. I am indebted to Daniel Duke for much of the analysis in the previous two paragraphs.

22. Roland S. Barth, "So You Want to Change to an Open Classroom," *Phi Delta Kappan*, LII (October, 1971), 97.

23. Sarason, Zitnay, and Grossman, op. cit., p. 63.

24. Seymour B. Sarason, *The Culture of the School and the Problem of Change* (Boston: Allyn and Bacon, Inc., 1971).

25. Barth, op. cit.

26. Daniel Purdom, "A Conceptual Model of the Nongraded School," doctoral dissertation, University of California, Los Angeles, Calif., 1967, pp. vii-viii.

27. *"Team teaching is a type of instructional organization, involving teaching personnel and the students assigned to them, in which two or more teachers are given responsibility, working together, for all or a significant part of the instruction of the same group of students."* (Italics in the original) Judson T. Shaplin, "Description and Definition of Team Teaching," *Team Teaching, ed.* Judson T. Shaplin and Henry F. Olds, Jr. (New York: Harper & Row, Publishers, 1964), p. 15.

28. Robert Anderson, "Some Types of Cooperative Teaching in Current Use," *The National Elementary Principal*, XLIV (January, 1965), 23. Anderson has added a seventh criterion not mentioned in the above article.

29. Lionel Elvin, "The Positive Roles of Society and the Teacher," *Perspectives on Plowden*, ed. R.S. Peters (London: Routledge & Kegan Paul, 1969), pp. 102-103. [U.S. publishers, Humanities Press, Inc.]

30. Louis M. Smith and Pat M. Keith, *Anatomy of Educational Innovation: An Organizational Analysis of an Elementary School* (New York: John Wiley & Sons, Inc., 1971), pp. 367-68.

31. Amitai Etzioni, *Studies in Social Change* (New York: Holt, Rinehart, & Winston, 1966), as cited in Smith and Keith, ibid., pp. 370-73.

32. Marilyn Hapgood, "The Open Classroom: Protect It from Its Friends," *Saturday Review*, LIV (September 18, 1971), 68.

33. "One of the problems of the open classroom in America today is that its advocates are too blinded by hope and jargon to see its problems as problems," ibid., p. 66.

34. Donald Orlosky and B. Othanel Smith, "Educational Change: Its Origins and Characteristics," *Phi Delta Kappan*, LIII (March, 1972), 414.

35. Sarason, Zitnay, and Grossman, op. cit., p. 42.

36. Arthur L. Stinchcombe, "Social Structure and Organization," *Handbook of Organizations*, ed. James G. March (Chicago: Rand McNally & Company, 1965), pp. 148-50. Reprinted by permission of Rand McNally College Publishing Company.

37. Sherman, op. cit.

38. Herbert R. Kohl, *The Open Classroom: A Practical Guide to a New Way of Teaching* (New York: A New York Review Book, 1960).

39. Barth, op. cit.

40. Robert M. Hutchins, "The Schools Must Stay," *The Center Magazine*, VI (January/February, 1973), 14. Reprinted with permission of *The Great Ideas Today, 1972* and Encyclopedia Britannica, Inc.

41. Barth, op. cit.

42. J. Cecil Parker and Louis J. Rubin, *Process as Content: Curriculum Design and the Application of Knowledge* (Chicago: Rand McNally, 1966), p. 2.

43. *The New School Science* (Washington, D.C.: American Association for the Advancement of Science, n.d.), p. 4.

44. Ralph Tyler, *Basic Principles of Curriculum and Instruction* (Chicago: The University of Chicago Press, 1950), p. 55.

45. Ibid.

46. Paul L. Dressel, "The Meaning and Significance of Integration," *The Integration of Educational Experience, the Fifty-Seventh Yearbook of the National Society for the Study of Education*, Part III, ed. Nelson B. Henry (Chicago: The Society, 1958), pp. 3-25. The yearbook includes twelve chapters, but Dressel's chapter is by far the most insightful and comprehensive.

47. Carl Bereiter, "Schools Without Education," *Harvard Educational Review*, XLII (August, 1972), 406.

48. Joseph J. Schwab, "Structure of the Disciplines: Meaning and Significances," *The Structure of Knowledge and the Curriculum*, ed. G.W. Ford and Lawrence Pugno (Chicago: Rand McNally & Company, 1964), pp. 1-30.

49. Kohl, op. cit., p. 52.

50. Hutchins, op. cit., p. 14.

51. Orlosky and Smith, op. cit., p. 414.

52. Mary Brown and Norman Precious, *The Integrated Day in the Primary School* (New York: Ballantine Books, 1968), p. 19.

53. Barth, op. cit., p. 70.

54. Ibid., p. 144.

55. Philip W. Jackson, *Life in Classrooms* (New York: Holt, Rinehart, and Winston, Inc., 1968), pp. 143-55.

56. Richard H. Hall, "Professionalization and Bureaucratization," *American Sociological Review*, XXXIII (February, 1968), 97.

57. Sam Leles, "Teacher Power—What's It All About?" *Theory Into Practice*, VII, The Ohio State University (April, 1968), 60-61.

58. Reprinted by permission of the publisher from Sloan R. Wayland, "The Teacher as Decision-Maker," in A. Harry Passow, editor, *Curriculum Crossroads*. (New York: Teachers College Press, copyright 1962 by Teachers College, Columbia University), p. 47.

59. George Denison, *The Lives of Children: The Story of the First Street School* (New York: Random House, 1969).

60. Orlosky and Smith, op. cit.

61. Sarason, Zitnay, and Grossman, op. cit., p. 90.

62. Bereiter, op. cit., p. 394.

63. Bereiter, ibid., p. 391.

64. Michael B. Katz, "The Present Moment in Educational Reform," *Harvard Educational Review*, XLI (August, 1971), 349.

65. Hutchins, op. cit., p. 16.

66. Donald C. Klein, *Community Dynamics and Mental Health* (New York: John Wiley & Sons, Inc.), p. 141.

67. Donald A. Myers, *Teacher Power—Professionalization and Collective Bargaining* (Lexington, Mass.: Lexington Books, D.C. Heath and Company, 1973).

68. Gerald Levy, *Ghetto School: Class Warfare in an Elementary School* (New York: Pegasus, Western Publishing Company, Inc., 1970), p. 41.

69. Ibid., pp. 42-44.

70. Barth, op. cit. p. 140.

71. Levy, op. cit., p. 176.

72. Barth, op. cit., p. xiv, "Introduction" by Joseph Featherstone.

73. Jonathan Kozol, "Free Schools: A Time for Candor," *Saturday Review*, LV (March 4, 1972), 52.

74. Levy, op. cit., p. xii.

75. Barth, op. cit., p. 156.

76. The conclusions draw heavily from the empirical study conducted by Myers and Duke, op. cit. While Daniel Duke may not agree with all of them, his contribution to the conclusions is substantial and it is a rare privilege to have had the opportunity to share ideas with such an insightful and brilliant colleague.

77. Orlosky and Smith, op. cit.

78. Donald A. Myers and Daniel L. Duke, "Elementary School Appraisal—The Status of Open Education in New York State Elementary Schools, 1971-1972," unpublished manuscript, p. 57.

Selected Bibliography

Selected Bibliography

Anderson, James. "The Authority Structure of the School: System of Social Exchange." *Educational Administration Quarterly*, III (Spring, 1967), 130-48.

Barth, Roland S. *Open Education and the American School*. New York: Agathon Press, Inc., 1972 © by Roland S. Barth.

_____. "Open Education: Assumptions about Learning and Knowledge." Unpublished doctoral dissertation, Harvard University, 1970.

_____. "So You Want to Change to An Open Classroom," *Phi Delta Kappan*, LIII (October, 171), 97-99.

_____, and Rathbone, Charles H. *A Bibliography of Open Education*. Newton, Mass.: Early Childhood Education Study, 1971.

Bassett, G.W. *Innovation in Primary Education*. A Study of Recent Developments in Primary Education in England and the U.S.A. New York: John Wiley & Sons, Inc., 1970.

Bereiter, Carl. "Schools Without Education." *Harvard Educational Review*, XLII (August, 1972), 390-413.

Bidwell, Charles E. "The School as a Formal Organization." *Handbook of Organizations*. Ed. James G. March. Chicago: Rand McNally, 1965, pp. 972-1022.

Blackie, John. *Inside the Primary School*. London: Her Majesty's Stationery Office, 1970. [New York: Schocken Books, 1971.]

Blyth, W.A.L. *English Primary Education*. 2 Vols. London: Routledge and Kegan Paul, Ltd., 1965.

Brown, Mary, and Precious, Norman. *The Integrated Day in the Primary School*. London: Ward Lock Educational Co., Ltd., 1968. [New York: Agathon Press, Inc., 1970.]

Bussis, Anne M., and Chittenden, Edward A. "Analysis of an Approach to Open Education." Interim Report of the Educational Testing Service, Princeton, New Jersey, August, 1970.

Cohen, David K. "Children and Their Primary Schools: Volume II." *Harvard Educational Review*, XXXVIII, No. 2 (Spring, 1968).

Collings, Ellsworth. *An Experiment with a Project Curriculum*. New York: The Macmillan Company, 1923.

Consultative Committee on the Primary School. *The Hadow Report: A Report of the Consultative Committee on the Primary School*. London: Her Majesty's Stationery Office, 1931. (Reprinted 1962.)

Cox, C.B., and Dyson, A.E. (Eds.). *The Black Papers on Education*. London: Davis-Poynter, Ltd., 1971. See especially: G.W.J. Crawford, "The Primary School: A Balanced View"; and D.M. Pinn, "What Kind of Primary School?" Black Paper Two.

Cremin, Lawrence A. *The Transformation of the School*. New York: Random House, 1964.

Denison, George. *The Lives of Children: The Story of the First Street School*. New York: Random House, Inc., 1969.

Dewey, John. *Democracy in Education: An Introduction to the Philosophy of Education*. New York: The Macmillan Company, 1916.

_____. *Experience and Education*. New York: The Macmillan Company, 1938.

_____. *The Child and the Curriculum*. Chicago: The University of Chicago Press, 1902.

_____, and Dewey, Evelyn. *Schools of Tomorrow*. New York: E.P. Dutton & Co., Inc., 1915.

Duke, Daniel Linden. "The Selling of the Open School." *The Journal of Educational Thought*, VII (April, 1973), 36-47.

Featherstone, Joseph. "How Children Learn." *The New Republic* (September 9, 1967), 15-19.

_____. "Report Analysis: Children and Their Primary Schools." *Harvard Educational Review*, XXXVIII, No. 2 (Spring, 1968).

_____. "Schools for Children: What's Happening in British Classrooms." *The New Republic* (August 19, 1967), 17-21.

_____. *Schools Where Children Learn*. New York: Liveright Paperbound Edition, 1971.

_____. "Teaching Children to Think." *The New Republic* (September 9, 1967), 15-19.

_____. "Tempering a Fad." *The New Republic* (September 25, 1971), 17-21.

Goodman, Paul. *Compulsory Mis-Education*. New York: Horizon Press, 1964.

Graubard, Allen. "The Free School Movement." *Harvard Educational Review*, XLII (August, 1972), 351-73.

Gross, Ronald, and Gross, Beatrice (Eds.). *Radical School Reform*. New York: Simon & Schuster, 1969.

Hall, Richard H. "Professionalization and Bureaucratization." *American Sociological Review*, XXXIII (February, 1968), 92-104.

Hapgood, Marilyn. "The Open Classroom: Protect It from Its Friends." *Saturday Review* (September 18, 1971), 66-69, 75.

Hechinger, Fred M. "They Can Be a Bit Too Open." *New York Times*, September 26, 1971.

Hutchins, Robert M. "The Schools Must Stay." *The Center Magazine*, VI (January/February, 1973), 12-23.

Informal Schools in Britain Today. New York: Citation Press, 1971. (23 Booklets).

Isaacs, Nathan. *Early Scientific Trends in Children*. London: National Froebel Foundation, 1958.

_____. *The Growth of Understanding in the Young Child*. London: Ward Lock Educational, 1961. [New York: Agathon Press, Inc., 1971.]

_____. *New Light on Children's Ideas of Number*. London: Ward Lock Educational, 1960. [New York: Agathon Press, Inc., 1971.]

Isaacs, Susan. *Childhood and After*. London: Routledge & Kegan Paul, Ltd., 1948. [New York: Agathon Press, Inc., 1970.]

_____. *Intellectual Growth in Young Children*. London: Routledge & Kegan Paul, Ltd., 1930. [New York: Schocken Books, Inc., 1966.]

_____. *Social Development in Young Children*. London: Routledge & Kegan Paul, Ltd., 1933.

_____. *The Children We Teach*. London: University of London Press, 1963. [New York: Schocken Books, Inc. © 1971.]

_____. *The Educational Value of the Nursery School*. London: Nursery School Association of Great Britain and Northern Ireland.

Jackson, Philip W. *Life in Classrooms*. New York: Holt, Rinehart, and Winston, Inc., 1968.

Katz, Michael B. *Class, Bureaucracy and Schools*. New York: Praeger Publishers, Inc., 1971.

Kilpatrick, William Heard. *Project Method: The Use of the Purposeful Act in the Educative Process*. New York: Teachers College, Columbia University, 1918.

Kohl, Herbert. *The Open Classroom*. A Practical Guide to a New Way of Teaching. New York: A New York Review Book, 1969.

Kozol, Jonathan. "Free Schools: A Time for Candor." *Saturday Review*, LV (March 4, 1972), 51-54.

_____. "The Open Schoolroom: New Words for Old Deceptions." *Ramparts*, XI (July, 1972), 38-41.

Levy, Gerald. *Ghetto School: Class Warfare in an Elementary School*. New York: Pegasus, Western Publishing Company, Inc., 1970.

Marin, Peter. "The Free School Nonmovement: Has Imagination Outstripped Reality?" *Saturday Review*, LV (July 22, 1972), 40-44.

Myers, Donald A. "The Humanistic School, A Critical Analysis." *The Educational Forum*, XXXVII (November, 1972), 53-58.

_____, and Duke, Daniel. "Elementary School Appraisal—The Status of Open Education in New York State Elementary Schools, 1971-1972." Unpublished Manuscript, 1972.

_____, and Klein, M. Frances. "Educational Programs—Elementary Schools." *Encyclopedia of Educational Research*. Ed. Robert L. Ebel. Fourth Edition. London: The Macmillan Company, 1969. Pp. 395-410.

Neill, A.S. *Summerhill: A Radical Approach to Child Rearing*. New York: Hart Publishing Company, 1960.

Orlosky, Donald, and Smith, B. Othanel. "Educational Change: Its Origins and Characteristics." *Phi Delta Kappan*, LIII (March, 1972), 412-14.

Passow, A. Harry (Ed.). *Reactions to Silberman's Crisis in the Classroom*. Worthington, Ohio: Charles A. Jones, 1971.

Peters, R.S. (Ed.). *Perspectives on Plowden*. London: Routledge & Kegan Paul, 1969. See especially Lionel Elvin, "The Positive Role of Society and the Teacher"; and Robert Dearden, "The Aims of Primary Education."

Piaget, Jean. *The Child's Conception of the World*. New York: Harcourt, Brace, and World, 1929.

_____ , and Inhelder, Barbel. *The Psychology of the Child*. New York: Basic Books, Inc., 1969.

Plowden, Lady Bridget, et al. *Children and their Primary Schools: A Report of the Central Advisory Council for Education*. London: Her Majesty's Stationery Office, 1966.

Rathbone, Charles H. "Open Education and the Teacher." Unpublished doctoral dissertation, Harvard University, 1970.

_____ (Ed.). *Open Education: The Informal Classroom*. A Selection of Readings that Examine the Practices and Principles of the British Infant Schools and their American Counterparts. New York: Citation Press, 1971.

Riordan, Robert C. *Alternative Schools in Action*. Bloomington, Indiana: Phi Delta Kappa Educational Foundation, 1972.

Rogers, Carl. *Freedom to Learn*. Columbus, Ohio: Charles E. Merrill Publishing Company, 1969.

Rogers, Vincent R. *Teaching in the British Primary School*. London: The Macmillan Company, 1970.

_____ . *The English Primary School*. New York: The Macmillan Company, 1970.

Roszak, Theodore. *The Making of a Counter Culture: Reflections on the Technocratic Society and its Youthful Opposition*. Garden City, New York: Doubleday & Company, Inc., 1969.

Sarason, Seymour B. *The Culture of the School and the Problem of Change*. Boston: Allyn and Bacon, Inc., 1971.

_____ , Zitnay, George, and Grossman, Frances Kaplan. *The Creation of a Community Setting*. Syracuse, New York: Syracuse University Division of Special Education and Rehabilitation and the Center on Human Policy, 1971.

Sherman, Vivian S. *Two Contrasting Educational Models: Applications and Policy Implications*. Educational Policy Research Center, Stanford Research Institute, Menlo Park, California, September, 1970.

Silberman, Charles E. *Crisis in the Classroom: The Remaking of American Education*. New York: Vintage Books, A Division of Random House, 1970.

Smith, Louis M., and Keith, Pat M. *Anatomy of Educational Innovation*. An Organizational Analysis of an Elementary School. New York: John Wiley & Sons, Inc., 1971.

Tuchman, Bruce W., Cochran, David W., and Travers, Eugene J. "Evaluating the Open Classroom." Paper presented at the Annual American Educational Research Association Conference, New Orleans, February, 1973.

The University of the State of New York/The State Education Department. "Open Education: Theresa, Theater, and Terrariums." Prepared by Jennifer Andreae and reviewed by Peggy L. Azbill and Ruth C. Flurry, n.d.

Walberg, Herbert J., and Thomas, Susan Christie. *Characteristics of Open*

Education: Toward an Operational Definition. Newton, Mass.: Education Development Center, 1971.

_____ . "Open Education: An Operational Definition and Validation in Great Britain and United States." *American Educational Research Journal*, IX (Spring, 1972), 197-208.

Weber, Lillian. *The English Infant School and Informal Education.* Englewood Cliffs, New Jersey: Prentice-Hall, Inc., 1971.

Zijderveld, Anton C. *The Abstract Society: A Cultural Analysis of Our Time.* Garden City, New York: Anchor Books, 1971.

Index

137

About the Authors

Donald A. Myers is head of the Department of Curriculum and Instruction, College of Education, Oklahoma State University. He received his bachelor's degree at the University of Nebraska, Omaha; his master's and Ph.D. at the University of Chicago. He has taught in the public schools, served in public administrative capacities, and taught in several universities. He is the author of numerous articles and several books, the most recent entitled, *Teacher Power—Professionalization and Collective Bargaining.* He is guest editor for an issue concerned with open education for the *Journal of Research and Development in Education.*

Lilian Myers is Editor of the *Capitol Hill Educator*, a publication concerned with the state legislative process and distributed to various agencies throughout the State of New York. She received her bachelor's degree in English at the San Fernando Valley State College in Northridge, California and her master's in Curriculum Planning and Development at the State University of New York at Albany. She has worked at the National Education Association, Washington, D.C. with Robert M. McClure and the late Ole Sand. She is the editor of an engineering handbook and has edited several published manuscripts and professional tradebooks in education.

Jenny Andreae was trained at the Froebel Educational Institute, University of London and has taught in both England and the United States. She has been consultant to many school districts implementing open education including two institutions with advanced programs—University of Connecticut and City College of New York. She has been coordinator and teacher-trainer of open classrooms in New Rochelle City School District and Croton-on-Hudson, New York, and has published several manuscripts on open education. She is presently Director of Advisory Service, the Teachers' Center at Greenwich, Connecticut.

Daniel Linden Duke received his bachelor's degree in history from Yale University, graduating Phi Beta Kappa and Magna Cum Laude. Currently completing his doctorate in Curriculum and Instruction at the State University of New York at Albany, he is conducting extensive research on the origins and development of alternative schools. He has written several articles on the growth of open education in the United States. He is presently an instructor of a course on "The Open School" at Russell Sage College in Albany, New York.

141

Mauritz Johnson has been a high school teacher and administrator and was a research associate with the New York State Education Department. Since 1953, he has been a professor at the State University of New York at Albany and at Cornell University, where he was also Dean of the School of Education from 1966 to 1968. He is the author of three books, the latest being *American Secondary Schools*. Among his numerous articles, one entitled "Definitions and Models in Curriculum Theory" has been reprinted several times since it appeared in *Educational Theory* in 1967.

Joseph Leese is Chairman, Department of Curriculum and Instruction at the State University of New York at Albany. Professor there since 1948, he has also taught in universities throughout the nation and at universities in Reading and Manchester, England, Bergen, Norway, and Hamburg, Germany. He is past president of the New York State ASCD.

A student of William Heard Kilpatrick and L. Thomas Hopkins at Teachers College, Columbia University, he participated initially in the Resource Use Movement in the South and guided a variety of experimental programs for exceptional children. His brochure on *Integrating the Elementary School* describes efforts to reorient the school day around children's interests and needs. He is coauthor, with Mauritz Johnson, of *The Teacher in Curriculum Making*, which explores the critical role of the teacher in the curriculum improvement process.